T0247976

Praise for
Forging Bonds in a Global Workforce

If you're looking to enhance your ability to connect and collaborate with colleagues from different cultural backgrounds, this book is an indispensable tool and a must-read.

—**Marshall Goldsmith**, Thinkers50 #1 Executive Coach and
  New York Times bestselling author of *The Earned Life*,
  Triggers, and *What Got You Here Won't Get You There*

This book is more than just a theoretical guide; it provides a practical road map for building and nurturing cross-cultural relationships in the real world.

—**Erin Meyer**, Professor of Management, INSEAD, and author
  of the bestselling book *The Culture Map: Breaking Through
  the Invisible Boundaries of Global Business*

I've been waiting for a book like this one. Andy and Melissa provide a fresh framework that is theoretically robust and immensely practical. *Forging Bonds in a Global Workforce* will be my go-to recommendation for people looking for help on what cultural intelligence looks like in the real world of work.

—**David Livermore**, PhD, Professor, Boston University, and
  author of *Leading with Cultural Intelligence*

In this engaging new book, Molinsky and Hahn provide powerful, practical approaches to developing the skills you need to thrive in our multicultural world. Solidly researched and full of relatable real-life stories, *Forging Bonds in a Global Workforce* is a much-needed guidebook for thriving in today's workplace.

—**Amy Edmondson**, Novartis Professor of Leadership,
  Harvard Business School, and author of *Right Kind of
  Wrong: The Science of Failing Well*

Building connections across cultures is an increasingly important skill. This book is filled with actionable, data-driven advice on how to do it more effectively. Wherever you work, you'll come away with some new ideas on how to bridge divides and build trust.

—**Adam Grant**, number one *New York Times* bestselling author of *Hidden Potential* and *Think Again* and host of the podcast *Re:Thinking*

An essential guide for every global professional. *Forging Bonds in a Global Workforce* moves beyond the tired narrative of "cultural differences" and provides invaluable insight and actionable strategies on how to foster trust and build meaningful connections in today's cross-cultural, digital world—with a focus on empathy and curiosity.

—**Amy Gallo**, author of *Getting Along: How to Work with Anyone (Even Difficult People)*

This book belongs on the bookshelf of any global leader—dog-eared and with lots of notes in the margins.

—**Mark Mortensen**, Professor of Organisational Behaviour at INSEAD and Owner, GlobalWorks Consulting

Forging Bonds in a Global Workforce is a magnificent guide to connecting across cultures, offering a comprehensive set of practical strategies for making and deepening diverse connections, in person and virtually. Grounded in research and rich with real-world examples, this engaging and accessible book is an invaluable resource for anyone working in a global context—and for those who have yet to do so!

—**Sally Maitlis**, Professor of Organizational Behaviour and Leadership, University of Oxford

As a global executive with teams across Asia, Europe, and the Americas, I will be providing this book as standard reading for all my leaders who work in multicultural teams across the globe and look forward to implementing some of the learning myself.

—**Yvette Bellamy**, Global Operations Executive Director, Boston Consulting Group

Whether the reader is new to an international team or an experienced professional, *Forging Bonds* will provide a valuable and timely compass to navigate the maze of creating effective intercultural relationships.

—**Donald F. Zyriek, II**, former Director of Operations at NXP Semiconductor, retired with 40 years in the global semiconductor industry

What sets this book apart is its focus on the practical aspects of understanding that people, not companies, drive global success. This is a must-read for individuals and groups in building cross-cultural relationships.

—**Karen Lynch**, Vice President Sales and Marketing, RJR Technologies

Whether you are an entrepreneur striving to enter a market overseas, a manager aspiring to get the most out of your geographically and generationally diverse team, or an educator trying to leverage the diverse lived experiences and cultural perspectives of your community as a means to elevate excellence, *Forging Bonds in a Global Workforce* gives you a framework and examples for thinking about the challenges and opportunities before you and offers pointed questions to reflect on how best to act upon your newfound knowledge.

—**José Luis Cruz Rivera**, PhD, President, Northern Arizona University

This book is more than just a theoretical guide; it provides a practical road map for building and nurturing cross-cultural relationships in the real world.
—**Xian Li**, former Head of Asia, Fox International Productions

Forging Bonds in a Global Workforce is a must for anyone seeking to navigate the complex and nuanced dynamics of international relationships.
—**Alice Lin**, Vice President & Senior Talent Advisor, Liberty Mutual Insurance

Everyone can benefit in their professional lives by adding the tools from this easy-to-digest book full of enjoyable scenarios and thought-provoking questions.
—**Keith Wexelblatt**, VP, Labor & Employment Law–Americas, Thermo Fisher Scientific

Building strong, trusting relationships—social capital—is the ultimate driver of success in business, finance, advocacy, politics, and careers of all kinds. Molinsky and Hahn's brilliant, accessible work unlocks the secret to forging strong relationships.
—**Steve Rochlin**, CEO, IMPACT ROI

FORGING BONDS IN A GLOBAL WORKFORCE

BUILD RAPPORT, CAMARADERIE, AND OPTIMAL PERFORMANCE NO MATTER THE TIME ZONE

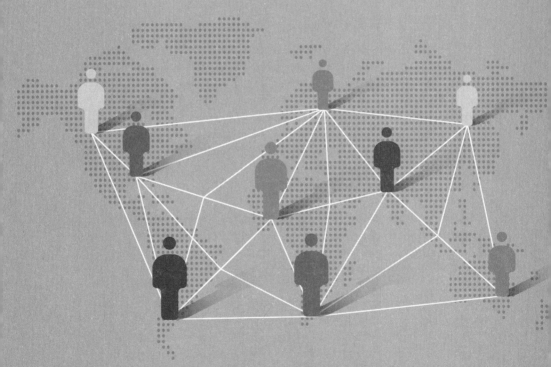

ANDY MOLINSKY & MELISSA HAHN

Mc Graw Hill

NEW YORK   CHICAGO   SAN FRANCISCO   ATHENS   LONDON   MADRID
MEXICO CITY   MILAN   NEW DELHI   SINGAPORE   SYDNEY   TORONTO

Copyright © 2024 by Personal Change Systems LLC and Melissa Hahn. All rights reserved. Printed in the United States of America. Except as permitted under the United States Copyright Act of 1976, no part of this publication may be reproduced or distributed in any form or by any means, or stored in a database or retrieval system, without the prior written permission of the publisher.

1 2 3 4 5 6 7 8 9   LCR   29 28 27 26 25 24

ISBN   978-1-265-21233-9
MHID   1-265-21233-3

e-ISBN   978-1-265-21490-6
e-MHID   1-265-21490-5

This publication is designed to provide accurate and authoritative information in regard to the subject matter covered. It is sold with the understanding that neither the author nor the publisher is engaged in rendering legal, accounting, securities trading, or other professional services. If legal advice or other expert assistance is required, the services of a competent professional person should be sought.
—*From a Declaration of Principles Jointly Adopted by a Committee of the American Bar Association and a Committee of Publishers and Associations*

McGraw Hill books are available at special quantity discounts to use as premiums and sales promotions or for use in corporate training programs. To contact a representative, please visit the Contact Us pages at www.mhprofessional.com.

McGraw Hill is committed to making our products accessible to all learners. To learn more about the available support and accommodations we offer, please contact us at accessibility@mheducation.com. We also participate in the Access Text Network (www.accesstext.org), and ATN members may submit requests through ATN.

To Alice, Ben, and Jen
—Andy

To my family
—Melissa

CONTENTS

SECTION 1
MINDSET

SECTION 2
BEGINNINGS

SECTION 3
DEEPENING

SECTION 4
FINER POINTS OF GLOBAL BONDING

PREFACE

Ron paced back and forth in his large office, overlooking a beautiful flower garden in downtown Washington, DC. He knew that this was perhaps his only chance to boldly achieve something his predecessors had never been able to do: create a trusting relationship with their bitter rival.

For years, the animosity between Ron's organization and its adversary had been simmering. In fact, competition was such a core part of their identity and purpose that he was initially intent on digging in—that is, until he surveyed the changing global landscape and realized the potential benefits of altering course. Now, the practical question was *how* to build a strong interpersonal relationship with his foe—a man named Michael who, like Ron, had also recently ascended to his leadership role. It was definitely a long shot, as there was little to no history of trust or cooperation to build on. This was going to take ingenuity and some global bonding magic.

At first, they met virtually, exchanging messages that revealed a shared willingness to engage, and the glimmer of hope that their interactions might bear some kind of fruit for both parties. Eventually, they met in person. Although the first meeting was supposed to last just 20 minutes, it stretched into an hour and a half. They even added an impromptu walk by the lake, which provided an additional opportunity for bonding and connection.

In our research, we discovered old photos of this meeting and were struck by the unusually warm, comfortable, genuine rapport between these two men. It was as if they were already friends, despite their longstanding rivalry. One of Ron's directors concurred: "The personal chemistry was apparent. The easy and relaxed attitude toward each other, the smiles, the sense of purpose, all showed through."

Over the months and years, the relationship deepened. They maintained regular communication and made additional visits—sometimes even bringing their wives along. And ultimately, their core values became so aligned that despite the history of their larger conflict, they were able to develop and enact transformational agreements that would otherwise never have been possible.

As you perhaps guessed, "Ron" and "Michael" are actually Ronald Reagan and Mikhail Gorbachev—the former American president and the former Soviet leader—who came from completely different worlds and yet managed to end a decades-long Cold War. It was extraordinary at the time, and even today provides a powerful example of what global bonding makes possible.

Fast-forward to our own era, and most of us aren't in a position where the stakes are quite so high. Even so, we can take heart knowing that we, too, can create meaningful global relationships that bridge differences and make a significant impact on our work and lives.

We just need to learn how. And that's what this book is about.

ACKNOWLEDGMENTS

(ANDY)

I owe a great debt of gratitude to my Harvard University PhD advisor Richard Hackman, who has influenced me professionally more than anyone else in my life. I think about him a great deal, especially when I'm starting a new project or when I come to a crossroads in my academic career. I always wonder what Richard would say, and that gives me a strong sense of conviction and direction. As I was thinking about this acknowledgment section, two stories about Richard came to mind. The first was how I started writing books in the first place. About 15 years ago, I was attending a research talk Richard was giving at MIT. I had done quite a bit of academic research on cultural adaptation and was toying with the idea of writing a book, but hadn't done much more beyond that.

The talk was in a large lecture hall, and as I entered the packed building, I saw Richard pacing around—barefoot—as he often did (he was quite a character). He came up to me, said nothing, took me by the hand, and led me across the lecture hall to introduce me to some random person sitting on the other side of the auditorium. "Melinda—you're an editor at Harvard Business

Publishing. You should publish Andy's book about cultural adaptation." It was definitely awkward, but I was also grateful. And in 2013 I did indeed publish *Global Dexterity*—my first book—with Harvard Business Publishing, and Melinda Marino was my editor. That kicked off my book writing journey that led to this book you have in your hands.

The second story about Richard was one that he told about a conversation he had with another eminent organizational scholar, Karl Weick. As the story goes, Richard and Karl were together in the back of an auditorium somewhere—likely at a national research conference—listening to a talk about organizational behavior. As Richard tells the story, he had an epiphany that day while listening to the talk and felt compelled to share it—right then and there. "Karl," Richard whispered, "You know the difference between us. You want to understand the world. And me—I want to change it."

My goal as an academic has always been to try to change the world—or more specifically, to equip people with the skills, insight, and courage to be able to change their worlds in a positive way. For years, I've gotten such pleasure out of how many people I've been able to positively influence with my first book, *Global Dexterity*, and have always wanted to continue the story by focusing on something that *Global Dexterity* didn't: building global relationships. That's the origin story of the book, at least from my end. And it's been a pleasure to work on it.

There are so many people I want to thank—but first and foremost has to be my coauthor and collaborator, Melissa Hahn. Melissa has been an absolute pleasure to work with. She's a perceptive thinker, a talented writer, and such a trustworthy and reliable person—which, to be honest, is the number one quality I look for in a collaborator. I've enjoyed working with Melissa so much on this project and would welcome continuing the collaboration into the future. As an aside, it's amusing to note that despite having worked together on this book and on a few other projects over the years, Melissa and I have never met in person. We once got about 20 miles from each other when I was in Los Angeles for a college reunion weekend . . . but that was about it. I know we'll meet in person one day—perhaps even before the book is published and you read these words.

Writing a book about global relationships has brought me back to so many of the cross-cultural connections I've had throughout the years. I think back to my time as an undergraduate student studying in Spain—and how scared I was to make a connection with anyone. I then think back to my time working and living in Paris—and how this experience was the complete opposite: I bonded with so many different people from so many different places. I was so taken by the experience of cultural adaptation, in fact, that it inspired me to pursue my PhD in the first place. I remember keeping a diary in broken French about all the amazing experiences I had—often trying to break them down analytically, like a would-be sociologist. That was so long ago, but writing this book made it feel like yesterday to me. What a treat that has been!

Someone in particular I'd like to thank is Kinga Białek, who I met through Melissa a few years ago as a potential collaborator on a certification course on my first book, *Global Dexterity*. Two years and more than 10 cohorts of students later, I have enjoyed getting to know Kinga so much. She is so insightful about culture and has taught me a lot—much of which has made it into this book. Of course, I also need to thank all the participants in our Global Dexterity cohorts—60 or so (and counting!) professionals from around the globe that have learned about Global Dexterity and incorporated it into their work. It's been such a pleasure getting to know them and working with them. They, too, have inspired so many of the ideas in this book.

Numerous people have graciously read earlier versions of this manuscript and provided invaluable feedback. I extend my gratitude to Sheila Pisman, Yael Gill, Kinga Bialek, Minna Franck, Steve Molinsky, Aaron Cruze, and Donika Sollova.

I also wish to acknowledge the many professionals who generously dedicated their time to be interviewed for this project. And special thanks to two exceptional research assistants, Mildred Delgado and Donika Sollova, both talented MBA students from Brandeis and Fulbright Scholars from (respectively) Nicaragua and Kosovo. Together, we interviewed over 100 people whose insights made their way in this book, both directly (in terms of the stories they told) and indirectly (in terms of background inspiration for the ideas we developed).

There are many other people who have played a crucial role in making this book possible. I would like to express my deep appreciation to our editor, Michele Matrisciani, whose insightful feedback and enjoyable collaboration have been invaluable. Additionally, I extend my thanks to the excellent production team at McGraw Hill who translated our manuscript into the spiffy new book (or digital book) you now have in your hands!

My heartfelt thanks also go to my extended family, including my always supportive and encouraging parents Judy and Steve, my brother Eric, my sister-in-law Serena, my in-laws Margaret and Dennis, and my sister and brother-in-law Amy and John. And I have to mention my dogs as well—Hazel and Josie—who definitely spent the most total hours working collaboratively with me, warming my lap, cleaning the computer screen (and my face) with their licks, and participating in one way or another in nearly all of the Zoom calls.

Finally, I want to thank my family—my amazing wife Jen and my two equally amazing children Alice and Ben. I am deeply grateful to them for their unwavering support, encouragement, and much-needed distractions and breaks. Ben provided sports-related diversions, Alice fed my reality TV fix, and Jen was there for anything and everything. I love them so much, and this book is dedicated to them.

(MELISSA)

The classic image of a writer is the lonely author furrowing her brow at the typewriter, surrounded by wadded-up drafts and stale mugs of coffee. I, too, spent countless hours hunched over my laptop, deep in my internal world, trying to wrangle my thoughts and then package them into words that others would hopefully find convincing. Sometimes, entire pages poured out of me in that magical state that psychologist Mihaly Csikszentmihalyi describes as *flow*. And sometimes, the ideas pipeline was hopelessly clogged by that old nemesis of writer's block. But no matter how the process felt in a given moment, I was never actually alone. In this section, I'd like to acknowledge the many people who made this book happen in big and small ways.

Above all, one person I could always be certain of was my coauthor, Andy Molinsky. The metaphor that feels most apt is of two people driving on a (yearlong!) cross-country road trip with a destination and deadline, but an imperfect map. You brainstorm various itineraries and plot a course, but at some point, it is just you and the open road—or in our case, *the blank page*. You are now buckled in and committed, and come what may, there is no turning back.

In this situation, you need someone by your side with a rare set of capacities: the temerity to start the journey to begin with, the resolve to see it through to the end, the intelligence to execute it well, the resourcefulness to respond to whatever challenges arise, the patience to cope with your own idiosyncrasies, and the sense of humor to infuse the voyage with joy. As night falls and you're still hours from your destination, you discover how valuable it is to be able to trust them to take the wheel—and for them to trust you, too. And if you're *really* lucky, not only do you arrive in one piece (or in our case, actually write a book!), but you want to do it all over again. Thank you, Andy, for inviting me on this adventure and making it so memorable.

While the process of writing this book was rewarding, the main goal was to have it published. Thus, I would like to thank our editor, Michele Matrisciani, and everyone at McGraw Hill who turned our manuscript into the book you now hold in your hands. Without this team, our ideas would have remained a concept without an audience, and so we are truly grateful.

I would also like to thank those who helped me become the kind of writer who was up to the task. At the top of my list is M. Clare Mather, who taught French composition at St. Olaf College. Even though this was a foreign language class—or perhaps, because of it—she helped me develop a clarity and structure that had eluded me to that point. Her question: "Melissa, what is it that you are trying to say?" and her command "Then say that!" remain touchstones two decades later. I likewise thank Marc Robinson, my Russian professor, who once critiqued a literature paper with a note that my ideas were compelling, but the labyrinthine logic was very hard to follow. Until that moment, I had naively assumed that if I splattered all my thoughts on the page, some sort of alchemy would transform them into a coherent essay. The lesson that good writing was a craft that took *work* (sometimes a lot of it) made me the writer I am today.

Even with this foundation, there is no substitute for another pair of eyes, and so I also want to express my gratitude to everyone who patiently let us bounce ideas off them, who read our drafts, and who provided constructive feedback. An extra special "thank you" goes to Sheila Pisman, Yael Gill, and Aaron Cruze for reading various drafts from cover to cover, sharing their honest reactions, and making suggestions about everything from the content and structure to the narrative and pacing. Your recommendations helped us target our attention to the most impactful areas for revision, while also providing the reassurance every writer craves.

Yet all the feedback in the world would not have sufficed if we had not also had the stories from our interviewees and research participants to form the backbone and muscle of the book. And so, we owe a very hearty thanks to everyone who sat down and shared their own insights and experiences. Your contributions were invaluable in helping us develop our framework and in producing a practical book with real-world relevance. We are also grateful to the many people who simply conversed with us during our teaching, training, coaching, and everyday interactions. Sometimes, the best stories appeared where we least expected them!

I also want to acknowledge the difference it made having the right people in my life behind the scenes, long before this book was a flicker of an idea. First and foremost, I thank my parents, Gary and Deborah Cruze, for nurturing my love of all things cultural and international, for encouraging me to spread my wings, and for trusting me that I'd somehow figure it all out. I also thank my grandparents: Eugene and Caroline Hughes, for blazing the trail in higher education and being the first to embrace seeing and learning about the world; and Jay and Fran Cruze, for being role models in tending your own garden and living life on your own terms. Thank you also to the Zyrieks, especially Lisa, for always being there, and to Don and Song Hahn for making space for your daughter-in-law and showing me another way to live. To Aaron and Becky: you are the best brother and sister that I could ever ask for. And to the friends who checked in and cheered me on, I appreciate you more than you know.

Last, but absolutely not least, my thanks and my heart go to Mike. I tried to warn you on our first date more than 20 years ago that I didn't intend to live a "normal" life, and I was overjoyed to learn that you didn't want that, either. Thank you for understanding me, for seeing the world with me, for walking Magda with me—and especially for being you. *Saranghae.*

INTRODUCTION

As she read through a batch of emails for the third time, Jane felt deflated. Exactly three months had passed since the kickoff meeting of her global team—and looking back, it was hard to believe now that at the time she had felt so much promise. As the head of product for a major consumer packaged goods conglomerate, Jane was tasked with the job to develop a new potential product in a category that the company was struggling in. The product needed to be globally competitive and was viewed by the very top leaders of the organization as one of the highest-priority initiatives at the company. Needless to say, this team had to succeed—for the sake of the company, not to mention Jane's own reputation and future.

And if any global team was going to work out, Jane had expected it to be *this one*. After all, she had done everything she could to prep the team about cultural differences—even hiring a top consultant to explain all the little predictable differences among her team members—which Jane felt would be very important to know, since half the team was from Asia and the other half from Europe and North America. The consultant had broken down the differences in indirect and direct communication styles, illuminating, for example, how Thomas, her German engineer, favored direct, to-the-point communication and how the Germans preferred "getting down to business" in meetings, rather than spending time with what they perceived to be inefficient, idle chitchat. The consultant also provided a handy list of potential trip wires—things to avoid—like publicly critiquing Japanese colleagues on the team, because it would make them lose face. And finally, the consultant had explained that people from some countries were like *peaches* and others were like *coconuts*—meaning some were easy to get to know at first but ultimately had a hard center, while others were difficult to get to know at first, but then once you were in, you were in for life.

Fortunately, from a timeline standpoint, things were operating relatively smoothly. The team had produced an initial prototype, which seemed to have promise. The problem was the group dynamics—in particular, the obvious lack of trust and connection among members of the team—which Jane feared could ultimately cause its downfall.

With this in mind, Jane had requested feedback from the team members about their experiences—and now felt deep anxiety and dread after reading just the first few: "The team feels like a group of strangers," one person wrote. Another said, "I'm not sure I really trust anyone here enough to provide the feedback that I really need to give." Another lamented that "there's no team spirit." And perhaps the most troubling of all was the incredibly nonspecific and exceedingly polite responses she received from her Asian team members. Instead of answering her question, they thanked her for the opportunity to contribute to this important product. For Jane, what was missing in these emails was just as troubling as what was present in the others.

As she reflected on her own attempts at bonding with individual members of the team, she understood the challenge. For example, she had tried several times to make small talk before virtual meetings—which even in the United States can be admittedly awkward. But with this particular group, it felt *especially* awkward. Jane would ask, in her typical friendly, upbeat tone, how everyone was doing . . . and she'd get complete silence. OK, sometimes maybe a "Good" from Thomas, the German engineer—but that was about it. *She could almost hear the crickets chirp.*

Jane considered herself a people person, and at least in the United States had never had much of a problem bonding with people and creating trust, even virtually. But bonding across cultures was clearly a different game. Jane knew that she had to figure something out—and fast. But from all the research she had done about cultural differences, not once had she found practical and useful resources for creating cultural connections—for bridging the gap and finding ways to build bonds across cultures in a way that would enable this team to reach its ultimate potential.

BEYOND CULTURAL DIFFERENCES

If you've ever read a book about global work or crossing cultures, you've certainly come across the idea of cultural differences. For example, you might have learned that Swedes are more individualistic than Chinese, or that Americans tend to schedule, arrange, and manage time whereas Mexicans and Indians are more apt to treat time more fluidly, being far less scheduled and guided by the clock. The unstated logic is that by focusing on differences, you'll avoid mistakes. And avoiding mistakes is the key to being effective across cultures.

There certainly is truth to this idea. This "cultural differences" approach was cutting-edge for the era it was created in—what we might call the Global 1.0 world—when few people were working across cultures or on global teams, when information about cultural differences was scarce, and when merely avoiding cultural mistakes was the coin of the realm. But the world has changed quite dramatically since the 1970s when this approach was developed. Today, nearly every major company is a global company. People routinely work across cultures in some capacity. And basic knowledge about cultural differences is readily available.

We completely understand if focusing primarily on cultural differences has been your go-to strategy for approaching global work. That's perfectly natural since it's how the field generally approaches the topic. However, what we have found—from our own research and practice as well as the interview project we conducted for this book—is that myopically focusing on differences can often get in the way of building relationships.

For example: when we are primed to think about differences, that might be all we ever see. In other words, we look for them, we find them, we catalog them, and we use them as a framing device for making sense of everything about that person and the situation. And when we have a limited amount of psychological energy to dedicate to thinking about culture and getting to know a new person, pouring all that energy into categories of differences can distort our perspective and prevent us from even considering alternative ways to engage with that person on our team.

Also, when we see another person primarily in terms of what makes them culturally different, it's not too big of a leap to end up exoticizing them or otherizing them, which means that we see them as a kind of perpetual outsider or other, not like us in some fundamental way. This can be dehumanizing to the person it is applied to, but it also has a distancing effect. It adds barriers to relationship building that you and the other person then must overcome—and then it's like you are starting from a deficit rather than just zero.

Finally, and perhaps most importantly, focusing exclusively or primarily on cultural differences can cause us to assume that the gulf between us and the other person is wider than it might really be—and may even lead us to think it is impassable. And when this happens, we may miss opportunities to find *commonalities* and *intersections*. This is not only counterproductive but probably contrary to how you build relationships within your own culture.

THE IMPORTANCE OF RELATIONSHIPS IN GLOBAL WORK

The reality of today's Global 2.0 organizations—like the one Jane helps to lead—is that people for the most part aren't struggling to merely *become aware of* or *understand* cultural differences (or if they are, they can easily grab useful information from books or the internet). Instead, people today need to be able to build effective cross-cultural relationships despite these differences. And rather than this being a skill set reserved for top talent in every-once-in-a-while, high-stakes, make-or-break business trips abroad, people at all levels of the organization need to be able to forge and sustain these global bonds, in person and virtually, individually and on teams, every single day.

Relationships are essential in so many ways. They foster trust and confidence between business partners, clients, and colleagues. When trust exists, it becomes easier to collaborate, share information, make decisions, and deliver feedback. In customer-centric industries, relationships with clients are essential. By cultivating strong relationships with global customers, businesses can build loyalty and enhance customer satisfaction. Satisfied customers are more likely to become repeat customers, provide referrals, and offer valuable feedback for product and service improvements. Finally, positive relationships within the workplace contribute to employee engagement and retention. When employees feel valued, supported, and connected to their colleagues and managers, they are more likely to be satisfied with and committed to their work environment.

Of course, relationships don't only support us professionally; they also enrich our lives on a personal level. When people have positive, high-quality relationships, they are more engaged and motivated and experience positive emotions. Indeed, researchers have found a connection between high-quality interactions in the workplace and increased oxytocin and serotonin levels—the hormones beneficial for improved well-being and overall better mental health. In other words, good relationships and connections make our lives better.[1]

We therefore submit that it is time for a revamped approach grounded in the experience of the millions of professionals who are striving to make these global bonds happen. Instead of focusing on differences, we need to see how people can bridge their differences to create the trust and rapport necessary to feel connected, engaged, and successful. And instead of focusing on how to avoid mistakes at all costs, we need to see how robust relationships can buffer people from the mistakes and faux pas that they will inevitably make.

To develop the insights that we highlight in the book, we interviewed over 100 professionals from around the world about how they approached relationship building.[2] The vast majority of stories we report in the book are actual events, as told to us by people we interviewed, albeit with a few details changed to protect anonymity. A much smaller percentage of stories do not come from specific individuals, but are anecdotes we crafted to reflect insights from several different people we interviewed.

We did these interviews in waves, and after each batch, analyzed the insights our informants provided with an eye toward identifying common themes and strategies as well as puzzles and inconsistencies that we aimed to untangle in our subsequent interview rounds.

We also consulted pertinent academic literature in psychology and organizational behavior as intellectual grounding for the insights we developed. Finally, we reflected on our own experiences of global bonding. For Andy, this includes living in Spain and working in France; many different global research team collaborations; consulting and speaking at global organizations; and more than 20 years as a full-time professor at an international business school teaching—and building connections with—a highly diverse classroom of MBA and undergraduate business students. Melissa, too, has had deep experience building bonds across cultures, including living in Poland; leading global, virtual teams and collaborating on projects across cultures; working at the community level as an ESL instructor and diversity dialogue facilitator; teaching American and international graduate students as an adjunct professor; and training global teams and coaching expatriate executives.

A WORD ABOUT OUR OWN CULTURES

Before we dive into more about what this book is, we want to acknowledge the obvious—that this is a book on building relationships across cultures in the global workplace that is written by two Americans. And not only that, but two white, highly educated, English-speaking Americans. Because of this, there is likely a lot of overlap in our cultural assumptions and reference points and things that we take for granted.

But as we'll discuss in the book, culture isn't just about the country you're born in. It's also based on the region you're from, and here we diverge quite a bit. Whereas Andy grew up and went to college in the urban Northeast, Melissa grew up in the suburban Southwest, went to college in the rural Midwest, and briefly lived in the South. Curiously, even though we both lived near Los Angeles as adults, we did so in opposite corners of the sprawling metro area, and nearly two decades apart. All of this means that our spatial orientations, centers of gravity, and experiences inside the United States are different, as are the cultures that we grew up around and studied among (and interestingly, neither of us is very familiar with the other's regional cultures).

We have different generational cultures as well—Andy is Gen X, while Melissa is a millennial. And you might have noticed that we have different genders, too: Andy is male and Melissa is female—a cultural identity that research consistently shows makes a significant difference in business settings in most countries.

That said, we certainly recognize that two Americans—no matter how different we may seem to each other—can't hope to have an omniscient perspective on the world. And so, we happily admit up front that we don't have all the answers for every situation or every person. (Frankly, that would be an extreme claim for anyone to make.) To compensate for this, and to ensure that our material is truly international, we made sure that the people we talked to came from as many different cultures as possible. We talked to people who aren't part of the dominant culture in their home or host country, as well as people who have lived and worked across multiple cultures and have their own syncretic global perspective. We talked to highly seasoned professionals at the top of their organizational ladders as well as younger and midcareer professionals. We spoke with people who work across cultures virtually as well as those who travel frequently or move and work across cultures in person. Basically, we tried to hit as many nodes as possible in the global work experience.

As we did so, we learned the specific norms for relationship building inside individual cultures and identified patterns that transcend culture. Our goal, then, was to transform that data into an easy-to-understand, user-friendly framework that we think will give you the best chance of success when working with a wide range of cultures in a diverse, global business context.

WHAT THIS BOOK IS (AND ISN'T) ABOUT

Let's start with what this book is *not* going to be. It isn't going to be prescriptive, offering plug-and-play formulas where you enter the input (for example, the country you're working with), and generate a bullet point list about exactly what you need to do. Of course, we all yearn for simplicity and want black-and-white answers, but the downside is that approaches like this start to buckle under the pressures of real life. People are complex and life is messy—especially when you also add in the demands, pace, and fluctuations of global work. And we believe that you need advice that factors that unpredictability and variability into the equation from the beginning.

It's also not a book about DEI—the US acronym for diversity, equity, and inclusion. For one thing, from what we can tell, the specific cultures and jargon of DEI seem to vary from place to place and be country specific—and although there may be common themes, what is relevant, urgent, or practical in one culture won't necessarily be meaningful in another. But beyond this, DEI initiatives tend to take place at the organizational level, and involve leadership buy-in as well as systemic changes in policies, practices, and procedures. By contrast, our focus is on helping individuals experiment creatively within their own range of motion. Essentially, we believe that relationship building across cultures is something that each person can start now, regardless of their company's programs.

And finally, although this book is about cross-cultural relationships, it is not about *all* relationships that have a cultural element. That would simply be too broad and would involve so many different lines of inquiry that we would never have this book ready to share with you. So, you won't find tips here about intercultural friendship, dating, marriage, or long-term intimate partnerships along those lines, nor about issues related to them like parenting.

So, if this book isn't going to be a guide to exactly what to do in every situation, a manual on how to avoid offending people or overhaul institutions, or advice on how to navigate thorny cultural issues with your in-laws, then what is it about?

Quite simply, this book is about increasing the odds of building strong, successful, productive, and hopefully even mutually enjoyable professional relationships with people who are different from you. Years ago, Andy argued in one of his *Harvard Business Review* articles that *companies* don't go global, *people* do. And this is still true today: global work ultimately involves *people*—and ideally people who get along with each other, who like each other, and who can trust and rely on each other are going to work better together. Our goal is to increase your odds for success in this critical endeavor.

HOW TO USE THIS BOOK

The book is arranged in four sections, roughly following the stages of developing a relationship.

First, we focus on *Mindset*—which is relevant anytime in the relationship-building process, but especially at the outset.

Mindset involves developing a keen awareness of the biases that can interfere with building relationships and learning the "code" for how the logic of relationship building differs across cultures.

Next, we focus on *Beginnings*—capturing those initial stages of creating a spark and trying to find common ground.

We then move to *Deepening*. You've done the initial getting-to-know-you dance, and now it is time for strategies that help you deepen the relationship with your colleagues from another culture.

Finally, we focus on *Finer Points of Global Bonding*—applying what we have learned to a team context and offering advice for managing your own internal experience and even navigating disagreement as you attempt to put our advice into practice in the real world.

While it is perfectly reasonable to read the book from beginning to end (which we think never goes out of style), you will find that we have arranged our ideas in bite-size chapters that you can peruse at your leisure. Although we have placed these in the order we think will be ideal for most readers—a flow from the first encounter with someone to the stage where you hopefully feel confident that a relationship is taking root—feel free to navigate our chapters in whatever way suits your needs best. You'll also find handy thought exercises at the end of most chapters to help you reflect on how the ideas we have introduced apply to your specific situation.

This book has been a labor of love for us, and we sincerely hope you enjoy it and find it useful in your personal and professional life. Let's get started.

SECTION 1
MINDSET

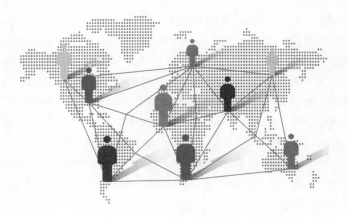

We have a confession to make. While both of us are knowledgeable about culture, cultural differences, and relationship building across cultures, neither of us is a terribly competent gardener. Melissa was never really exposed to gardening, as she grew up in Phoenix, which has a hot desert climate like Riyadh's. Andy, on the other hand, is from Boston, where the climate is ideal for growing many things . . . but he just never got into it. Why do we bring this up? *Because growing a garden is a great metaphor for building relationships across cultures.*

The gardening gurus we consulted suggest that there are two main ways to cultivate a flourishing garden. The first is by avoiding the "bad stuff" that makes a garden fail. This includes things like planting in poor sunlight, choosing the wrong plants for your soil, or failing to create a barrier between your plants and weeds. These are things *to avoid* if you want to increase the odds of growth. But of course, avoidance-based strategies alone aren't enough. You also need to *do* the "good stuff" to help the garden grow and thrive. You need to water your plants. You need to feed them compost and fertilizer. Certain plants need to be pruned.

Hopefully, you're getting a sense of the metaphor here. Creating the conditions for a relationship to grow is like creating the conditions for a garden to blossom. You need "avoidance-based" strategies to dodge pitfalls plus a corresponding set of "growth-based" strategies to nurture the relationship. You want to avoid needlessly offending the other person, but you also want to do something to make them want to connect.

With this metaphor in mind, the first section of the book focuses on mindset—how you can train yourself to avoid potential pitfalls and misunderstandings that can all too easily short-circuit a relationship before it gets off the ground.

FOUR CRITICAL ERRORS

There are four critical errors to avoid to keep from sabotaging good cross-cultural relationships: fixating on national culture, stereotyping instead of prototyping, assuming other people are like you, and reducing relationship complexity to "peaches and coconuts."

ERROR #1
Fixating on National Culture

Andy has never been more surprised when meeting someone than he was when he met Huaxing Chen, the CEO of a Singaporean consulting firm who wanted to see if they could collaborate on some projects. As Andy recalls:

> Huaxing was traveling to Boston, where I live, and asked if we could meet up. I honestly didn't think much about the meeting ahead of time, and as I walked up the stairs that hot summer day, I was expecting someone very different from the person I ultimately met. My assumption was that a Singaporean CEO would likely be serious, businesslike, guarded, and formal. As soon as I saw the huge smile on Huaxing's face and heard his friendly booming voice, I realized he was nothing like the person I imagined. *I actually thought he was going to hug me!*

When we think about culture, many of us immediately think about *national culture*—that is, the country a person comes from. And that is understandable. National culture is an easy identifier in the global workplace—as in, our team includes three Israelis, four Malaysians, two Nigerians, and one Colombian. It isn't wrong to observe and contemplate this. The trouble comes when you make two related assumptions: (a) that the most important thing about another person is their national background, and (b) that they will likely act a certain way based on your assumptions about that background.

For one thing, your understanding of their national culture is probably incomplete, and shaped by whatever biases people in your home culture have of that country, or by what you might have picked up and then half-remembered from movies and television. But more important is the simple fact that many elements *other than* the country we are from also shape our behavior and mindset. Or putting it a different way, sometimes national culture is the main actor, sometimes it is the supporting actor, and sometimes it is a red herring.

Let's look first at how even something as seemingly straightforward as "what country you're from" can actually be more complex than you might think. Consider the fact that some people are from more than one country—perhaps because their parents came from two different countries, because their family has immigrated, or because they hold dual citizenship. Melissa encountered this on a recent global team training that she led for a multinational conglomerate. When she spoke to the team manager ahead of time, he told her that his employees were based in the United States, Brazil, Poland, India, and China. However, when Melissa met the team during her first live session, it turned out that the person in the United States was Vietnamese American, the person in Brazil was half Italian, one person in Poland was Ukrainian, and the other was Turkish (and he wasn't even physically in Poland but was working remotely from Germany)! In a situation like this, focusing on national culture alone could easily lead a person astray.

There are also those who grew up across multiple countries, not because they changed their citizenship but because their parents' jobs took them overseas. This might sound like the exception rather than the rule, but when you stop to consider that kids with global childhoods are more likely to pursue global careers as adults, this increases the odds that someone in your global office probably has a more complicated cultural backstory than you'd initially think.

We should also bear in mind that sometimes it's not the country that matters most, but the region. This was certainly the case for Sung-ho Choi, a South Korean executive from Seoul who has lived, worked, and traveled across China for many years. When we interviewed him about the cultural differences he had observed between South Korea and China, his immediate question was, "What part of China?" The reason, he explained, is that China is an enormous country that contains many regional variations. And according to him, one of the most noticeable differences was not just between South Korea and China (as he had anticipated), but between Shanghai and Beijing within China.

Specifically, he recalled that what he viewed as "Western-style" small talk was much more common in Shanghai. And this makes sense if you consider the context: Shanghai is an international business hub with one of the world's busiest ports. It hosts multinational companies and thousands of expats with a wide range of global backgrounds. It also attracts young Chinese professionals who have lived, worked, and studied abroad in Western business schools where they became familiar and comfortable with Western-style relationship-building norms.

By contrast, he found Beijing to feel a bit more traditional. Here, you also have international businesses, expats, and students, plus globally educated Chinese professionals. However, historically the real center of gravity has been the government, which gave the city a different cultural flavor—one that was more local and administrative than cosmopolitan and innovative. To our South Korean colleague, this difference was palpable, even as an outsider. Accordingly, he had to adjust his way of approaching business conversations and relationship building, not just because he was in China, but depending on where he was in the country.

Finally, although it might initially seem counterintuitive, a person's national culture may ultimately be less significant in global work than their industry, organization, profession, and job function. While we don't want to stereotype these categories, either, we have probably all met people who seem like a quintessential engineer, real estate agent, professor, doctor, accountant, sales executive, or pilot. And inside a company (say, a global auto manufacturer), the biggest gap might not be between the Germans, Mexicans, and Americans, *per se*, but between operations, sales and marketing, design, production, and quality control or customer service. Each department may have its own values, priorities, way of working, and lingo—and even in the same organization with the same customers, they may approach the job very differently.

The point we want to emphasize is that while national culture is likely relevant, you often can initially tell very little about an individual person by their national culture alone. National culture is an indicator of what someone from a particular culture *might* be like—but it is a rough one at best. It is possible that a person will be just like you imagine. But there's also a good chance they won't be—or that as you get to know the real them, beneath the national culture surface, they will surprise you in ways that you never expected.

ERROR #2
Stereotyping Instead of Prototyping

It was happening again—and Lucy Harris couldn't believe it. Lucy was in Houston with her colleague to pitch a business proposal to a major potential French client, Dr. Hélène Duval, who had flown in from Paris for a weeklong series of visits to the United States. This was a critical pitch for Lucy's firm, since they had just started landing major international clients and developing a reputation for their work outside the Americas region. If they could sign this particular client, Lucy believed, it could open the door to the French market—and then perhaps more of the European Union. That is . . . if Lucy's partner Doug Gordon had even *an ounce* of cultural competence.

Frankly, it would have been a lot easier if Lucy could have done these meetings solo—and she sorely wanted to suggest it this time. But Doug was the quantitative specialist, and they anticipated that Dr. Duval would ultimately be swayed by the numbers. Lucy figured that if Dr. Duval had questions, they had better have quick answers, and Doug was great at that. She just wished she could count on his people skills. Gritting her teeth, Lucy walked into the meeting with Doug alongside—hoping for the best but fretting about whether this really *was* for the best.

The meeting started off fine with a few cordial hellos, but then it went downhill—fast. Doug, perhaps in a misguided effort to be respectful and accommodating to his foreign guest, started speaking very . . . slowly . . . and . . . deliberately, reminiscent of how you might speak to a child or an elderly person who was hard of hearing. "We . . . are . . . so . . . happy . . . that . . . you . . . can . . . meet . . . with . . . us, . . . Dr. . . . Duval." It went on for about 30 cringeworthy seconds, but for Lucy it might as well have been 30 minutes. She wanted to slip off her chair and melt into the floor.

Doug's miscalculation was clear the moment Dr. Duval started speaking—in crisp, fluent, BBC-style English. "It's a pleasure to meet you both, too. But before we begin, I just want to clarify: Doug, is it OK for you if we continue in English? I am comfortable, of course—if you are."

When doing business with people from different cultures, we're often understandably focused on the content of the business itself. For example, in the case above, Lucy explained to us that they had pulled multiple all-nighters getting ready for this visit—detailing information about the potential market, outlining the parameters of a collaboration, and understanding the technology at Dr. Duval's firm and how it might align with the expertise Lucy and Doug were building. So, they certainly weren't lazy or ill-informed about the work itself.

The problem was that they put all their eggs into the hard skills basket without adequately considering the soft skills side—in this case, the intercultural dynamics of the meeting. Now, we can't know for sure where Doug's stereotype of Dr. Duval came from. But one thing we do know is that stereotypes are one of the most important things to avoid when cultivating your cross-cultural relationship garden. One reason is that when people sense that they are not being seen as themselves, but rather as a stereotype the other person has created in their mind, it tends to diminish their enthusiasm for pursuing the relationship. Yet preconceived ideas don't just cause offense to the other person. Stereotypes also short-circuit our own imaginations, freeze our curiosity, and end up severely restricting our ability to think and see beyond our own expectations. In this way, Doug's stereotyping hindered him and led him astray.

We all probably understand what stereotyping is: assuming someone is characteristic of our image of the group they belong to. So, if you are about to meet an Italian, and you think Italians are emotionally expressive, you will assume that the person you are about to meet is emotionally expressive, too. That is logical enough—but it could also be wrong.

In contrast, whereas *stereotyping* is a naive, blunt, and often hurtful way of approaching cultural differences, *prototyping* is nuanced, sophisticated, and constructive. It acknowledges that cultures have norms and tendencies at the population level, but also invites us to anticipate variety at the individual level. Sticking with our Italian example, a prototype is the average in a population—in other words, the "average" Italian. Imagine you could snap your fingers and create a perfectly accurate graph of all Italians in terms of their level of emotional expressiveness. On this graph, the prototype would be right in the middle. Knowing this information is useful because it gives you a rough idea of where *most* Italians might fall. But you still need to keep in mind that any *particular* Italian you meet could fall anywhere on the graph. They might be "prototypical" and conform to exactly what you guessed. But they could also be somewhat less expressive than the norm, or somewhat more expressive—or even much more expressive! You simply don't know in advance. Chances are, if Doug had prototyped instead of stereotyped in the situation above, he likely would have had a much more successful outcome.

ERROR #3
Assuming Other People Are Like You

Imagine the following: You're an extroverted person from a culture where people make small talk freely and easily. We know that for some of you, this will be very hard to imagine. (And maybe you are already fantasizing about how to escape from this scenario.) But if you can, try to picture this and imagine that chatting with people is one of your favorite things to do.

You love the give-and-take, and the fast-paced, stimulating rhythm of conversation energizes you like an exciting tennis match. You can't seem to get enough, so you intentionally surround yourself with other extroverts. In fact, one of the things you love most about your sales job for a retail startup is how personable and outgoing everyone on your team is.

Now, picture a twist. You find yourself on an SAS flight to Helsinki to source new materials and designs for your company. And you're feeling especially enthusiastic because this is your first big international trip—and after all, you love meeting new people.

The plane lands early in the morning Helsinki time. You have a quick coffee (or two) at the airport, hop into a taxi, and make your way to your downtown meeting. You walk into the room to greet your Finnish counterparts by name (which you practiced on the plane to make sure you got the pronunciation *just right*) with a big grin (thinking of going in for the hug) and . . . *silence*. Well, not total silence. A brief, cold hello muttered without much of a smile at all. No small talk. No asking about your flight. No comments about the snowstorm that has just started or jokes about whether you'll be warm enough. No remark on how it's so great to finally meet in person.

You think to yourself: *This is so awkward*. Your counterparts look awkward, too: just sitting there, drinking coffee all by their lonesome, not knowing what to say. They must feel like this is the most uncomfortable interaction ever, too. You almost feel sorry for them.

However, if you knew anything about Finnish culture, you would realize that this isn't out of character for the country. Finns typically don't make much small talk, and they are generally quite comfortable with silence. (As one of our Finnish colleagues explained, "We just don't feel an obligation or need to fill time and space with words.") You thought you sensed that they were feeling uncomfortable and awkward as they sipped their coffee solitarily, but they weren't at all.

It turns out that you were doing what psychologists call *projecting*:[1] since we can't literally peek into the minds of the people we're interacting with, we often (lazily) just assume they must be thinking and feeling and experiencing the same things we are—because, after all, that's the information that is available to us in our minds. It's what we know. And it just seems to make sense.

Of course, if you really think about it, it doesn't make much sense at all. Why should someone from a different culture with a different background, mindset, and worldview think, feel, and experience something just like we do? Projection limits our ability to shift perspective—to step into the shoes of the other person for a moment and consider their view on what's happening and how they might interpret and make sense of our behaviors and their own. And we frequently fall prey to this trap because we don't recognize that (a) there is a cultural logic to relationship building, (b) the person across the table from us is probably operating according to a different logic, and (c) we are also bringing our own cultural logic to the table. As a result, when someone acts in a way that is different from what we expect, we interpret that behavior through our own cultural lens. And this can unfortunately compound misinterpretations and misunderstandings.

For example: You're late for a meeting and assume that the person you're working with is really upset at you. Why? Are you assuming this because you know them and have heard them grumble about how people waste their time by arriving late? Or are you stressed because you know that *you* get upset with people who are late, so you assume they will be, too? If it's the latter version, that's projection. What if the person comes from a culture like Brazil's, where timeliness isn't typically as highly prized as in Switzerland? Or what if they are a very laid-back person who just isn't that clock-oriented? In either case, they might not be upset at all!

ERROR #4
Reducing Relationship Complexity to "Peaches and Coconuts"

Experts in culture and global work often use metaphors to help translate fuzzy and abstract concepts into concrete and user-friendly images. This can be beneficial in some respects but can also lead us astray or lock us into unhelpful assumptions. With this in mind, one that raises our own hackles is "the peach and the coconut." Just as Jane learned from her consultant, the idea is that people are from cultures that are either "peach-like" or "coconut-like" in terms of how quick and easy it is to get to know them. In peach cultures, it's easy to build a quick rapport by piercing the soft outer flesh, but much harder—if not impossible—to build a meaningful, authentic connection because eventually you reach a hard center (symbolized by the pit). By contrast, in a coconut culture, you see the reverse: it takes a long time to penetrate the hard outer shell—but once you do, you have access to the full interior world of the person (the coconut meat and juice)—and thus, a true friend for life.

The metaphor is popular and appealing because it reduces a very complex topic into a catchy heuristic. It conveniently removes the messiness of ambiguity and individual differences—*you're a peach or a coconut, and that's that.* It also supposedly helps you predict or explain the other person's behavior and approach to relationship building. (Why is the American on the plane telling me her whole life story? *She must be a peach—it all makes sense now!* Why is that Russian so hard to get to know? *He must be a coconut—that's why.*)

Unfortunately, this kind of thinking can pull us into stereotyping instead of prototyping. Do you really think that all 330 million-odd Americans are peaches (the United States is often touted as a peach culture) and all 80 million Germans (the classic coconut culture) are indeed coconuts? We doubt it. Not to mention that the metaphor unravels the more you chew on it. For example, you obviously can't eat the pit of a peach—so does that mean you can never build a deep or lasting bond in a peach culture? This would seem to imply that certain cultures are superior and inferior when it comes to relationships—a judgment that doesn't match our research and experience, and that frankly makes us uncomfortable.

But most important for our purpose is that it's not instructive or actionable. Even if you enjoy imagining two categories of relationships that resemble these fruits, the question that still arises is what to do with this information. How do you actually go about forging a bond with people in the global workplace? (Once I label myself a peach and you a coconut . . . then what?)

If we must use food as a metaphor for relationship building in a non-stereotypical way, we prefer the notion of a spice blend. Just like the name implies, a spice blend has many different individual spices that contribute to an overall flavor. Some specific spices can be stronger and more influential than others, and some may even accentuate or cancel out others. For example, you might think that a blend with basil in it will taste a certain way—that is, until you taste it and realize it's actually the rosemary or peppercorn that dominates the flavor.

Similarly, applying this now to culture, you can know that someone is from France, but it might turn out that their ultimate behavior—how they present themselves—may be very different from your assumption of that single characteristic. That's because there are other things in their personal "blend"—like their professional background, their experiences living and working in other cultures, their personality, or their role in the situation. And somewhat paradoxically, this may actually be *more* confusing if you have had previous experience with France—say you've worked with French people before, have perhaps enjoyed elements of French culture, and have maybe even been to France yourself. Perhaps Doug has visited France, and while he was there, observed that locals would not speak in English to him. So, he made what seemed to him a natural conclusion—that French people don't speak English—and then applied it to Dr. Duval.

When the most pronounced flavor of the person's style isn't what we anticipate, it can feel disorienting. But rather than thinking that their style is wrong, it's a chance to reframe our approach to that person—to consider what other "spices" make up their unique blend and which ones might be the most potent in our specific workplace dynamic with them. And we can imagine what a difference it might have made for Doug to take this approach!

HOW THE FOUR ERRORS INTERFERE WITH RELATIONSHIP BUILDING

Of course, you may not necessarily fall prey to all these errors. But even one or two can seriously interfere with relationship building. Remember: You're seeing *their* behavior through *your* own cultural mindset, as well as your own personality and past experiences. And if you're focused and fixated on differences, and the negative impression you're developing of this person is only accentuated by the fact that you see them in stereotypical terms— as characteristic of how people from their culture "always" act— then you aren't getting to know the real person at all.

The process can be confusing and frustrating. You can feel annoyed at the other person and annoyed with yourself. And you might feel resentful or impatient that your interaction is hard or confusing. In this state of mind, it's very easy to draw inaccurate conclusions about the other person's behavior. These feelings can then leak into how you act.[2] You can appear distant or peevish—perhaps not obviously so, since you're trying to suppress these feelings—but it might very well be obvious to the other person that something is up, as research suggests that we aren't so great at hiding our emotions. And even if you do manage to mask them, negative feelings can still cause you to become demotivated, withdraw, or avoid. After all, who wants to persist in doing something that isn't pleasant or doesn't seem to be pay-ing off? The result can be that you detach from the other person—and then they also detach from you. You each show a bit less interest and motivation to work on the relationship, and as a result, the relationship goes nowhere. In other words, it stalls.

We capture this process in Figure 1.1, starting up top with behavior that you (1) consider confusing or unexpected. For example, imagine you're meeting someone from Brazil—and you "know" (or think you know) that Brazilians are very outgoing. But what if this *particular person* disconfirms your expectation? That creates cognitive dissonance for you, which (2) triggers a negative attribution or interpretation of what you consider to be their "weird" behavior. You (3) feel uncomfortable and experience negative emotions because the rug was ripped from under your steady expectations. You probably (4) decide that this relationship isn't for you, which further influences your subsequent negative interpretation of their behavior. It's likely that this all happens instantaneously and unconsciously, in a split second. And it creates quite a hill for the relationship to climb for it to be successful.

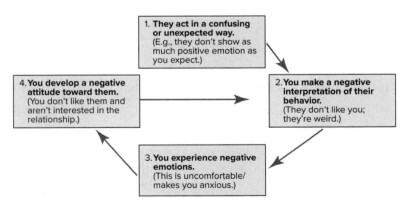

FIGURE 1.1 The dysfunctional consequences of faulty cultural sensemaking.

And by the way, the very same thing might be happening on their end—about you! They might be expecting *you* to act in a certain way, based on their biases about what they think your culture is like or even because of their own projections. And when you disconfirm their expectations, a similar negative spiral of attribution, emotion, and withdrawal of interest occurs. All in a split second, likely without them being aware of this beneath-the-surface process, either.

You see the challenges here. The cultural differences involved can cause the relationship to short-circuit even before it gets off the ground—not because the differences themselves are necessarily insurmountable, but because our minds instantly leap to conclusions based on our inherent biases about what these differences mean. And once we arrive at these meanings, it sets us on a path that leads us away from each other.

So how can you build successful global connections in light of these challenges? In his book *Thinking, Fast and Slow*,[3] eminent psychologist Daniel Kahneman describes two different modes of thinking: System 1 thinking, which is fast, instinctive, and emotional (along the lines of the biases we just described), and System 2 thinking, which is more deliberate, effortful, and logical. Our goal here is to help you correct slippery System 1 thinking and introduce a more System 2–style mindset that enables you to become more informed, intentional, and open-minded about what you are observing and what you make of those observations. The good news is that you can start developing this ability now, by noticing the biases we just outlined and by mastering the logic of relationship building that we introduce in the next chapter.

MASTERING THE LOGIC OF RELATIONSHIP BUILDING

(AKA THE 6 P'S)

Maria Hernandez was so excited to finally be going to Tel Aviv. She had been working for a water purification startup in Mexico City for about a year now, and so far, all communication had been via email, phone, Slack, and Zoom. Now, Maria was getting the chance at last to meet her colleagues Orit, Aron, and David in person. She was hoping to get a better sense of who they were as individuals and to deepen her connection with them so they could work even better together after she returned home. And of course, the trip had an important business angle, too: the joint venture with the Israeli side had exceeded expectations, and Maria would now lead a strategic brainstorming session about where the company was headed.

After arriving in Tel Aviv and taking a night to recover from the 20-plus-hour journey, Maria took a taxi to the office. On the way, she admired the sunny Mediterranean city out the window, noting things she might mention when making small talk. After all, she wasn't sure what, if anything, she would have in common with the Israeli team, but complimenting their city seemed like a safe way to gently ease into conversation. Soon, the moment had arrived: she was meeting her colleagues face-to-face. As they shook hands and greeted her vigorously, she felt enveloped by their hospitality.

However, to Maria's shock and dismay, the goodwill she initially experienced evaporated almost instantly. Orit, Aron, and David bypassed small talk niceties completely, and instead started shouting at each other (and her!) in what felt like a total free-for-all. Maria felt under fire whenever she opened her mouth, as everything she suggested was met with a forceful critique: *This was wrong! That was wrong! This idea was stupid! That idea would never work!* And it was delivered with such intensity that Maria almost wanted to cry. She had never experienced anything like this dynamic—it was certainly nothing like the good-natured, constructive, supportive dialogue she had with her coworkers back home. (At least at home, people had the decency to say something positive before just shooting you down!) But more than the heat of the moment, it was what that heat implied that really jarred Maria. How could she have so grossly miscalculated the nature of her relationship with her Israeli colleagues? And how would she ever be able to work with them again, now that she saw what they were really like?

This may sound counterintuitive, but it's likely that Maria had not miscalculated the relationship at all. In fact, her Israeli colleagues likely had a completely different experience and interpretation of this scene—and they might have been stunned and even horrified to learn that Maria had interpreted their interaction so negatively. To them, it might have simply felt like a robust discussion between close work colleagues—one that felt refreshingly authentic and productive, since they could finally interact naturally and spontaneously without having to accommodate technology issues like Zoom forcing them to speak one at a time. To Maria, however, this wasn't a thrilling way to converse at all, but rather made her want to hightail it back to the airport. Their completely divergent experiences can be directly attributed to the gap in their relationship codes.

As we discovered during our research, different cultures can have divergent implicit or unspoken rules and rhythms for relationship building. This means that people working together from different cultures may instinctively rely on different underlying assumptions and expectations about the getting-to-know-you and working-together process without even realizing it. Unfortunately, as we saw with Maria, the resulting feeling of being tangled up in knots can lead us to interpret the situation negatively—or even assume that it is hopeless or futile. But as we'll discover in the pages ahead, this may not be the case at all—and by learning how to decipher the relationship code, not only will we gain a better sense of what we're encountering in the moment, but we'll also be better equipped to respond in a way that is less stressful, is more satisfying, and helps us accomplish our big-picture work goals.

We capture these key cultural differences in a schema that we like to call the 6 P's (Figure 2.1). *In our experience, the 6 P's are at the heart of the confusion, misperception, and misattribution that can occur when people attempt to build relationships across cultures.*

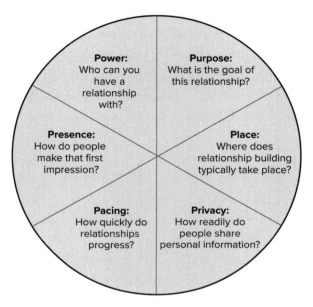

FIGURE 2.1 The 6 P's of bonding across cultures.

Some of the P's have to do with relationship building in general, or within a particular culture. Others have to do with the specific relationship in question. And just a friendly reminder: Although many of our examples in this book feature national cultures, make sure to keep in mind that regional cultures, organizational cultures, professional cultures, and so on can be just as influenced by these P's.

- **Power: Who can you have a relationship with?** In high power-distance cultures, there typically is a barrier between those at the top and those at the bottom of a hierarchy, and people may feel it is important to stay on their rung of the organizational ladder. In these cultures, it's normally difficult, if not impossible, to cross the barrier, especially from the ground up. On the other hand, there are also cultures that have almost no social distance between the top and bottom of the hierarchy—and in these, it's not just appropriate but expected and encouraged that people have relationships up and down the ladder.

- **Purpose: What is the goal of this relationship?** Is it purely personal? Instrumental? Transformational? Or a combination? Some relationships are clearly instrumental: the relationship is a tool for gaining personal or professional rewards. In other cases, the relationship is more about intrinsic personal benefit and enjoyment. And a third kind of relationship might be transformational—like a mentorship. Of course, some relationships can have more than one of these goals.

- **Place: Where does relationship building typically take place?** In some cultures, there are particular places and times that are most optimal for relationship building. And in others, relationship building might take place here, there, and everywhere.

- **Privacy: How readily do people share personal information?** In some cultures, there is a thick wall between one's private life and professional life. Picture a castle with a moat, a drawbridge, and maybe a series of concentric inner walls and courtyards. In other cultures, it's more like a wide-open garden where everything is on view. What you see is what you get! And of course, some cultures are in between, and it may depend on the context.

- **Pacing: How quickly do relationships progress?** In some cultures, relationships are a 50-yard dash, while in other cultures they are a marathon walk or even a meandering stroll. And there might be different assumptions about how long-lasting and durable the relationship will be as well.

- **Presence: How do people make that first impression?** Cultures have different "typical styles" that are expected and appropriate when interacting in the workplace. This includes things like how formally to act, how directly to communicate, and how much positive emotion to exhibit. Of course, since this is also related to personality, this category is particularly subject to individual nuances and idiosyncrasy.

Let's have a closer look at each of these six dimensions of relationship-building logic in the pages ahead.

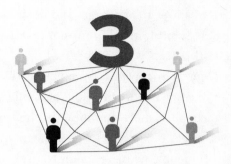

POWER

WHO CAN YOU HAVE A RELATIONSHIP WITH?

I n certain cultures, there are boundaries around who you can build a relationship with and what those relationships will look like. But the catch is that these limits aren't necessarily announced. There is no memo you're given about the people you can and can't have a relationship with. If you're an insider of the culture, it's obvious because it's something you've been taught your entire life. For example, in Japanese corporate culture, it would be highly unusual for a junior worker to approach a senior colleague and attempt to get to know them on a personal level. They might very well have a working relationship—but it likely would be highly formal, deferential, and polite, and most probably initiated and steered by the superior. This is because Japan is a hierarchically oriented culture where, as a child, you learn to show great respect and deference to elders—in your family, at school, in religious contexts, and then ultimately at the workplace.

The United States, by contrast, is a much less hierarchical culture—and relationships up, down, and diagonally across organizational levels are much more common. In this environment, a junior employee might actually need to show that they can initiate a rapport with people who are senior to them—for example, by making breezy small talk with the boss when they both end up in the same elevator, or by engaging in banter with the leader of another department before an all-hands meeting. Of course, hierarchy still matters—it's not like every junior person has dinner at the CEO's house on a weekly basis! But since the United States is less hierarchical than Japan, you have relatively more latitude to build relationships here. And moreover, demonstrating that you are capable of confidently crossing that power boundary is an important sign of your potential.

So far, so good—but what happens when you go from one cultural logic to another? Carl, a Canadian who works for a Japanese multinational, told us a story that illustrates the impact of power distance on cross-cultural relationship building. Carl is a senior manager who reports to an even more senior Japanese boss. Now, Carl was already aware of the strict power dynamics in Japan, and so he basically accepted that he was unlikely to develop a strong personal relationship with his boss like he might have expected to do with a Canadian one. But Carl still wanted to win her respect—so he was patient and waited for the boss to drop a hint that such a relationship might even be possible. And in Japan, Carl understood that this could take quite a long time.

Four years of working together passed without even a shred of personal connection. Then one day, his boss just happened to mention that she had to miss a meeting because of a commitment to play golf. To Carl, this minor personal detail screamed out as a key opportunity. Like a fisherman who has waited hours for a fish to bite on the line, Carl swiftly but dexterously reeled in the chance to ask a follow-up question about golf. Now, if you knew nothing of the cultural dynamics, that interaction likely would have seemed completely mundane or trivial. But in Carl's retelling of the moment, it turned out that this little detail and comment ended up being a pivotal point in the relationship. From that time on, they were able to get closer to each other and build a deeper, more trusting connection—not just because Carl had seized the moment, but because his boss had presented it to him in the first place.

Let's look at another example. Manuel is a Mexican professional who began reporting to a Texan boss after a global energy conglomerate bought first a Houston-based company and then one based in Villahermosa, Mexico. Manuel initially struggled to feel comfortable with his new boss, Rhonda, because she not only spoke casually to him but expected him to do the same with her. She even seemed a bit annoyed when he approached her in a deferential, hesitant, or polite way—she would brusquely wave her hand on the Zoom call and say, "You know I don't stand on ceremony, Manuel! Just spit it out!" On one level, it was exciting for Manuel to have a boss that wanted him to be himself—to stand up, speak up, and engage as a quasi-equal. He would never have done that with his boss in Mexico, and it felt invigorating and novel. But the problem was knowing exactly what establishing rapport up the hierarchy in an egalitarian way looked like. How exactly should he "just be himself" when talking to his superior? Should he ask about her family? Make a joke? Use slang? He was in uncharted territory: the boundaries that he was accustomed to had dissolved, but he sensed that other, invisible ones might have taken their place.

Of course, it's not just national cultures that can vary in terms of these power dynamics of relationship building. Organizational and industry cultures can as well. Imagine, for example, a super-lean startup launched by a few 20-somethings with a fresh idea and some initial capital. Now, place this company anywhere in the world—perhaps in a hierarchical country like China, Bangladesh, Tunisia, or Russia. Our hunch is that most tiny, early-stage startups would (a) tend to have somewhat similar power dynamics as each other and (b) tend to be less hierarchical than the national culture. Now, let's imagine a completely different type of organization, this time a high power-distance one like the military, and situate this organization in a relatively low power-distance country like the Netherlands or Sweden. Our guess is that in this case, too, organizational culture would trump national culture so that relationship building in the Swedish or Dutch military would be relatively more hierarchical than the "typical" organizational culture in that country. (Of course, if you are reading this from a garrison in Sweden or the Netherlands, enjoying beers and laughing with your commander, let us know and we'll stand corrected.)

A THOUGHT EXERCISE

- Does power influence who you can easily have a relationship with in your culture, or what those relationships might entail?

- How comfortable would you be having a relationship with someone higher or lower in an organization than you?

- What kinds of unspoken rules do people typically follow about power when building relationships?

- And what happens if these rules are broken?

PURPOSE

WHAT IS THE GOAL OF THIS RELATIONSHIP?

In some cases, relationships are purely instrumental—a means to an end. A good example of this is a large company in the United States where employees form cross-functional teams seemingly at a moment's notice, and then disband just as quickly once the short-term project is complete. Because the company is so large, once they get reassigned to a new team, they're unlikely to bump into former teammates again. In this context, being friendly and reliable pays off, but investing in a deep personal relationship doesn't. It would take too long at the outset, would be impossible to maintain at the project's conclusion, and wouldn't meaningfully advance the objectives. However, it doesn't mean that the people engaged in instrumental relationships see them as artificial, phony, or manipulative. Quite the opposite: they are transparent, pragmatic, and efficient.

In addition to being instrumental, some relationships can have a strong personal component as well. One example comes from China, where people often build their network of professional connections (*guanxi*) via a lengthy trust-building process during which they get to know potential associates on a personal level. This is not because Chinese professionals are necessarily more personable than the American team members mentioned above, but because here the character of your connections reflects on you, with consequences for your own social standing.

Moreover, since relationships are perceived to be enduring with mutual responsibilities, you have a vested interest in vetting potential associates beforehand. It typically takes many meetings and conversations—often over meals and not directly related to business at all—to develop a deep sense of familiarity, ease, and trust on a human level. It may also require subtle inquiries behind the scenes where you ask mutual acquaintances for their own insights and assessments about the other party. In this initial, protracted relationship-building dance, you are carefully scanning for signals about whether you can trust this person, if they have good character, and so on. If all goes well, you may eventually feel confident and comfortable enough to do business together.

If you were unfamiliar with this process and the purpose behind it, you could easily make multiple mistakes in interpretation along the way. For example, if you came from a culture where business was primarily instrumental, you could be confused about why these getting-to-know-you conversations and events were happening in the first place. Perhaps, you might conclude that the person wasn't interested in business at all since the conversation never veered in that direction. Or you might think that the person wasn't professional, or that "they don't get it." And that could make you frustrated, confused, and disappointed when the reality is that you simply misread the intended purpose of the relationship—and thus the relationship-building process leading up to it.

Likewise, if you were accustomed to patiently nurturing personal relationships, you might completely misinterpret the other party's instrumental style. You might feel bewildered or resentful that your counterparts want to get down to business and aren't interested in who you are as a person. You might also feel suspicious about potential reasons for their haste. Are they trying to push you into an agreement before something about their background comes out? Are they signaling that they don't intend to stick around for the long haul? Are they simply unseasoned and immature? Any of these misinterpretations could lead you to question the other people's professionalism and demotivate you from forging a bond.

Although the two examples above centered on national culture, we want to underscore the fact that even inside countries, relationships are not one-size-fits-all but can be situation-dependent. An interesting example about conflicting views of purpose within a culture comes from a Finnish interviewee who shared the anxiety that a Finnish person might have if a coworker invited her for coffee *outside the office. Inside the office* wouldn't raise any yellow caution flags, because Finns regularly have coffee together at work (even if, as we learned earlier, they don't necessarily talk a lot!). But once you leave those four walls and go outside the office for coffee with a coworker, it alters the meaning and purpose of the relationship—potentially dramatically. An invitation like this suggests that the person considers you a possible *friend* and is hoping to move in that direction. This is significant, because friendship in Finland is deeply meaningful and comes with long-term obligations—more like a family member than casual acquaintance. As a result, a Finnish person might feel ambivalent and conflicted, and even decline to participate in this otherwise innocent-seeming coffee date, because they can't shoulder the additional responsibility. It's not hard to imagine how a colleague from an instrumental culture might easily misunderstand all of this, because they wouldn't have any intuitive sense that they were changing the purpose by changing the place. But a person from a culture where the purpose of relationships is personal could just as easily be confused. If your whole goal is to get to know someone personally, you would likely not guess that getting to know them outside the office was too personal. As a result, you might again take this difference personally, when it really boils down to purpose.

A THOUGHT EXERCISE

- Can you think of a situation in your culture where the goal or purpose is purely instrumental?

- Can you think of a situation in your culture where the goal or purpose is purely personal (and not instrumental)?

- And can you think of a situation in your culture where the relationship purpose is a combination of these?

PLACE

WHERE DOES RELATIONSHIP BUILDING TYPICALLY TAKE PLACE?

I n some cultures, relationship building can take place in micro-moments virtually anywhere—in the parking lot or the elevator while you're walking in or heading out, in the conference room before a meeting, in the hallway when you pass by each other, in the break room as you're getting water or refilling your coffee, or when you happen to pop into someone's cubicle or knock on their office door. Because relationship building is fully integrated into the workplace and workday, we call these "integration-based" cultures. And in these cultures, there is very little perceived need for designated relationship-building time after hours.

A good example of an integration-based culture is the typical US office. Here, those working in person sprinkle "face time" and small talk into their interactions throughout the day by chatting around the watercooler, knocking on their boss's door with a quick question, or dropping by their coworker's station to "run something by them." If their company wants to promote team building, this usually takes place during the day—perhaps with a potluck lunch, where each employee contributes a dish to a communal meal. Some American organizations do have extra-curricular opportunities for engagement like a kickball team (like baseball, but you kick a large bouncy ball), but the assumption is usually that after-hours "fun" is optional. As one person said to us, "I've just spent eight or more hours with these people. In the evening, it's 'me time.'"

In contrast, there are other cultures where socializing is *not* typically built into the workday at all. Here, when people come to work, they work—and to them, "work" means completing their assigned tasks quietly, devoid of extraneous talking. One example of this kind of culture is Germany, where people are polite and proper, but don't tend to see the office as a place for making friends. In fact, Germans typically tend to draw a thick line between their personal and professional lives. So, although they don't talk much at the office, they aren't typically going out afterward, either.

In other cultures, the workday is reserved for work (that is, completing tasks), but relationships still matter quite a bit. In these cultures, there is a code for when and where relationship building takes place—and it's critical in these "separation cultures" to know this code and take advantage of the relationship-building contexts that do occur. There seem to be quite a few of these cultures, as you'll see from our stories that follow.

For example, Andy experienced this back when he was an intern at a French consulting firm in his early twenties. As he recalls:

> I remember being surprised by the lack of informal chatter in the office during the day—it felt so oddly stoic and cold compared to what I had experienced during my internship experiences in the US. That is, until the lunchtime break, when everything suddenly shifted. *En masse*, the entire office would trek down to the cafeteria together for a lunch of multiple courses, including wine and dessert! The vibe was leisurely and personable. People took their time to enjoy the food and conversation. They talked about their lives outside work (something I rarely if ever heard upstairs in the office). It was clear that relationships were being forged. That is, until we exited the café and assumed our original workplace positions and demeanor. The dichotomy was so odd to me at the time. But I've come to realize that this pattern is quite typical in a "separation"-type culture.

Likewise, our interviewee Ashley reports that her entire team at an office in Belfast takes tea and lunch breaks together—every day. (It is even outlined in her employee handbook.) Her office has a cafeteria like the one in Andy's building, and all her coworkers sit together, whether they bring a lunchbox from home or purchase a hot meal. Melissa asked her what would happen if she didn't join in, and she had this to say:

> I guess people would understand if you had to take care of something from time to time. But if you regularly

didn't join in with everyone else, it would probably affect your relationships negatively. For one thing, you'd miss out on getting to know them because they don't really visit each other's cubicles to chitchat at other times. But it would also send a signal that you didn't want to be with them, and they'd take it personally.

As it happens, many cultures have specific, designated places and times for relationship building—and while these often involve food, they can also revolve around activities. In Finland, it's not uncommon for colleagues to unwind at the sauna at the end of the week to bond in a more casual, informal atmosphere. (And unlike an off-site coffee, this comes with no strings attached.) In England, it's the pub after work, where colleagues—often across levels of hierarchy—bond together over rounds of beer, darts, and billiards. In South Korea, this may take place at a restaurant for a lavish and alcohol-soaked meal—or alternatively, at the golf course. Work teams are even known to go hiking in the mountains or engage in other outdoor recreation together. In Japan, it's the karaoke bar—where the more permissive atmosphere allows people across hierarchical levels the leeway to speak far more freely and openly than they would ever do in the workplace. But the next day, it's as if it never happened. (As Carl explains, the silence the day after a group night out reminds him of the slogan "What happens in Vegas, stays in Vegas.")

Of course, there are also cultures where there is little, if any, boundary between one's work relationships and one's personal relationships. For example, our colleague in Brazil told us that she would regularly text a coworker on the weekend to see if they wanted to check out a museum exhibition, go to the beach, or come to her children's birthday parties—and the assumption was that this coworker would say *yes* most if not all of the time. And we similarly heard from our interviewee in India that it is not uncommon to be invited to a coworker's wedding, or the wedding of their child, or to a gathering at someone's house to celebrate one of India's many religious festivals. These invitations are key opportunities for relationship building—and if you decide not to go without a very good excuse, you could end up inadvertently harming the relationship. The logic here is that you don't turn off relationships with people just because of the calendar or the clock. Bonding can happen anywhere.

As you can see, the space for developing relationships varies widely between cultures—and this means that our assumptions from our home culture not only are *not* universal but might even be the opposite of those held by our global coworkers.

A THOUGHT EXERCISE

- Are there particular places where professional relationships tend to be built in your culture?

- How would you feel about building relationships in the other ways that were described?

- How would it be received by your coworkers if you opted out of invitations or activities?

PRIVACY

HOW READILY DO PEOPLE SHARE PERSONAL INFORMATION?

In certain cultures, it may be quite common to bring your personal life to work. You might share stories about your weekend, hobbies and interests, family life, travels, and even your trials and tribulations. This might happen at random times throughout the workday, at lunch, or during a coffee chat. There is little, if any, separation between the public and the private; in this culture, it's important to reveal your "real" self to bond with others—to show that you are human, accessible, authentic, congenial, and open. Here, talking about yourself is professional.

In other cultures, it is just as important to keep your personal life separate from work—and in fact, to do otherwise could be viewed as "unprofessional." People here may make circumspect, polite conversation and potentially develop a trusting collegial relationship, but it's not a highly personal one that emerges primarily from knowing the intimate details of each other's lives. And this certainly isn't how you would start when initially getting acquainted.

In Germany, for example, it generally takes a while to feel comfortable enough with a new work colleague to share personal information. Germans often wait for a long time before even using the more familiar form of the pronoun "you" (*du*)—defaulting instead to the more formal version (*sie*) until the time is right. Considering this, divulging actual personal details would certainly feel, well, much too personal! And you wouldn't expect others to share, either.

One of our interviewees told a story about how this German style of personal disclosure created misperception and miscommunication during a corporate merger. The story took place at an American company that was purchased by a larger German firm. Suddenly, its American employees—who had little knowledge or experience of German culture—had German bosses with German expectations for relationship building (or the lack thereof). The American employees were turned off and disillusioned by their new German bosses, whom they experienced as cold, unfriendly, and uninterested in getting to know them as people.

A German boss might enter an American office to say hello, but that was literally it—a hello. There was no small talk, no friendly conversation—nothing. On the German side, the idea of building these quick, personal connections wasn't even on their radar. Their goal was to bring everyone up to speed as efficiently and quickly as possible. It didn't even occur to them that their American employees might yearn for a personal connection forged through sharing. Eventually, with cultural awareness training, the two sides came together, but this key element of personal disclosure was a real sticking point early on to building a successful working relationship.

Another example comes to us from a colleague who is Taiwanese and whose global career has included long-term assignments across Asia, Europe, and North America. While hopscotching between countries, she has encountered different approaches to disclosure—some that suited her and some that did not. In fact, from her cultural perspective, it is very uncomfortable to share personal information up front. To her, questions about where she is from, who is in her family, and so on are far too intrusive for an initial conversation.

To someone in the United States or other parts of the world, this might be very surprising and a bit of a head-scratcher—how else are you supposed to get acquainted if it isn't by asking questions? Her answer: "Talk about the food." As she explained, food is a common denominator that allows you to get used to the other person and share space together without necessarily revealing anything about yourself—at first. "You can ask the other person where a good place is for lunch, and that lets them show their expertise. You can talk about where you went for dinner last night, if you're in town for a business meeting. And that shows you are interested in their culture. You can ask them to eat with you, and then you can talk about the food you are eating. But you don't talk about yourself right away. That's for later—when you already know each other."

At the complete opposite end of the spectrum, our Brazilian interviewee said that the people she knew would find it frustrating for someone to deliberately avoid sharing about themselves, saying, "What is the big deal? We are all just people!" She explained that when they encounter someone who is guarded about details that don't seem to matter all that much, it can plant a seed of suspicion about why they are trying so hard to keep others at arm's length. "When we talk about our lives—even things that are difficult, like our kids are struggling in school, or we are annoyed at our partner for something—it shows we are relatable. It gives the other person a chance to listen, to offer advice, and to commiserate. If the other person doesn't share or let us in, we feel demotivated." She added that for Brazilians, personal information facilitates professional work, too. "If you're having a bad day, maybe I can help you finish your projects—and then, on another day, if I need help, I know you'll help me." In other words, the act of sharing in this culture boosts teamwork and helps them get the work done faster.

As you can see, there are significant differences in terms of how quickly people share information about themselves, and what they consider appropriate and useful to share, period. And it's not too hard to imagine that if you put a person from a sharing culture together with someone from a non-sharing culture, or if you are in a conversation asking innocent questions that the other person thinks are just way too intrusive, you might end up feeling like ships passing in the night.

A THOUGHT EXERCISE

- What's the balance between the personal and the professional in the work cultures you're a part of?

- What kind of personal information is considered normal or expected for people to share with coworkers?

- What is considered too personal to share?

PACING

HOW QUICKLY DO RELATIONSHIPS PROGRESS?

Some cultures and people rapidly develop an initial, surface-level trust, and that's enough for them to quickly get down to business. Meanwhile, others might be slower to build trust—and in some cases, may not be ready to do business at all until a sturdy foundation of trust is fully established. When you have a mismatch in your expectations of how quickly relationships are built, one party might feel rushed while the other may wonder what the holdup is. And this misunderstanding can stymie cross-cultural relationships before they even get going.

In Jordan, for example, building new business relationships takes quite a bit of time because personal trust is so essential to the entire process. And here, you can't fast-track trust. This was definitely the case for our interviewee from Japan, Daisuke Sato, who described his experience establishing a rapport with his Jordanian business partners as incredibly (and frustratingly) slow—at least compared to his experience building relationships in other parts of the world. And this was especially fascinating to us given our previous chat with Carl—who, as you'll recall, described the Japanese relationship and trust-building process as being exceedingly slow!

To us, this illustrates two key points. First, individuals can and often do vary in terms of their relationship-building styles, even within the same culture or country. And it is possible that Daisuke had a different style from that of Carl's Japanese boss—perhaps because of his personality, his industry, his profession, or even his extensive experience living and working abroad.

Second, differences are relative. For example, in the United States you could inquire about someone's spouse or partner after only a minute or two of getting acquainted. It's not a sensitive question—and it's certainly not taboo! In Japan, it would likely take longer—and you might need to find a particular time and place for that discussion (say, after work over a few drinks). You probably wouldn't just blurt out your question upon meeting them for the first time. But in Jordan, it took *10 months* for Daisuke to build up the level of trust necessary to ask questions about his business partner's wife. This is partly because, in Jordan, someone's female family members are an extremely private topic, reserved for people who have achieved a very high level of trust within the context of an established relationship. As you can see, the perception of what is normal, fast, or slow depends on where you and your culture fall on the continuum.

This is important because when we encounter significant differences in pacing, we might not know how to interpret them, and the resulting confusion may undermine our attempts at building a relationship. For example, our interviewee Hannah grew up in Austria before emigrating to Canada—where she discovered a huge difference in how quickly relationships blossomed. She recalls being caught off guard one day when she overheard a colleague refer to her as a friend. "Friend!" she declared to us, incredulously. "How can we possibly be friends? I have only known her for a few years!"

Hannah saw the humor in the story and told it with a laugh. She knew enough about Canadian culture to know that her colleague meant no harm, and that from her perspective, calling someone a "friend" was akin to saying, "You seem nice, and I have known you for a while." But now that she was aware of this mismatch in how each person classified the relationship, it hung in the air and started to color how she approached her colleague. "Now I feel awkward when we run into each other, so I try to avoid it. Because I always think, here comes that person who thinks we are really friends. And I don't want to encourage her."

While pacing can clearly impact global bonding between coworkers, it can also play a part in launching new business partnerships. Consider an American executive we interviewed—Steven Ruddy—who was in Finland for three days hoping to finalize a major consulting contract for his small marketing research firm. And because Steven knew next to nothing about Finland, he did something pretty smart: he hired an expert to provide him with insider knowledge about how to navigate relationship building with his Finnish colleagues. And his coach predicted a very interesting (and for Steven, quite unexpected) relationship trajectory.

At first, the coach said, the Finnish side would probably be all business—polite, but emotionally unexpressive. They likely would not start up any of what Steven considered "real" conversations—especially not the friendly, lighthearted small talk that Steven was familiar and comfortable with. However, after a few days of relatively dry and restrained presentations, meetings, and work dinners, there would be a critical tipping point: at the farewell dinner, his Finnish colleagues would likely let down their guard and talk Steven's ear off. At the eleventh hour, the coach predicted, they would flip their style, become convivial and personable, and the conversation, dinner, and drinking would last for hours. And it turned out that this is exactly what happened!

Steven shared that without his coach's prior insights, he likely would have misinterpreted his colleagues' early behavior as signs of disinterest or even rudeness—because that's what those signals would have meant in Steven's culture. And he might have been so bewildered or alienated that he didn't stick it out to the finish line. But since he *did* know what to look for, he could let the process flow along in due course—and as a result, he reaped the fruits of his labors and returned home not only with a signed contract, but also with several new business relationships.

The pacing of relationship development is clearly not universal, but in our minds, the potential *stages* in a relationship are. Around the world, people move from not knowing someone at all . . . to knowing them a bit . . . and then to potentially becoming acquaintances . . . close colleagues . . . or even friends. Of course, the exact progression across each of these stages may be culturally specific—and even personally specific in the sense that individuals have their own preferences and tendencies for how they build relationships. Remembering our spice blend metaphor, although the exact flavor may be a bit different, the general recipe still applies.

A THOUGHT EXERCISE

- Is relationship building for you like running downhill on an open road, or like navigating an obstacle course, where progress is possible, but at each stage it takes time and effort?

- Is there a particular "tipping point" for you where relationships either stall or significantly advance?

- And how about national culture? Is it possible to say whether there is a typical pacing of relationship development within cultures you're familiar with?

PRESENCE

HOW DO PEOPLE MAKE
THAT FIRST IMPRESSION?

What is the first impression you make on someone else when you meet them? And what do you pay attention to in terms of the impression that another person is making on you? These characteristics are part of our *presence*—and these first impressions can create a lasting impact. In fact, psychological research suggests that these quick, immediate impressions predict our subsequent longer-term impressions with startling accuracy.[1] The challenge for building relationships across cultures is that expectations and norms for these immediate impressions vary—often quite significantly. Three particularly relevant aspects of presence when it comes to relationship building across cultures are *enthusiasm, formality*, and *directness*.

ENTHUSIASM

When you meet someone for the first time, what's the immediate vibe you get? Do they smile, show excitement on their face, and greet you in an inviting, warm, upbeat, positive tone? Or are they more stoic, showing little expressed positive emotion? Of course, personality matters here a great deal, too—people who are more extroverted will tend to show more immediate, positive emotion than those who are introverted. But don't dismiss the power of culture.

Generally speaking, for example, Chinese professionals are often not particularly enthusiastic or emotionally expressive in business interactions. It's just not the dominant cultural norm. Instead, modesty, self-control, and reserve are key values in Chinese culture, and displaying too much outward enthusiasm, especially in front of a boss, can be seen as "showing off" or being "immature"—neither of which is professional. As one of our Chinese interviewees explained, there is still a deeply ingrained view that wise people are quieter. "If you are talking your mouth off, it gives the impression that you don't have that much going on inside your head." That said, Chinese professionals, of course, do express themselves—it just happens over time as they get to know a person. Additionally, as is the case in many countries, the younger generation tends to be more comfortable with emotional expressiveness than previous ones.

On the other hand, countries like Mexico, the United States, and Brazil are famous for having cultures that are more outwardly enthusiastic and emotionally expressive. And even though there are regional differences in each country, the general expectation would be that you'd introduce yourself in a workplace setting with a smile and be greeted with one in return. Here, a little frisson of energy sends an important message: *I am nice, I'm likable, I'm normal, I'm easy to work with—and we'll get along well!* Initial enthusiasm isn't usually viewed as superficial, but as an essential rapport-building ingredient—and if it's missing, it signals that something is likely amiss. Indeed, when people from enthusiastic cultures don't get at least a little enthusiasm in return, their minds start reaching for explanations—none of them good. *Is the other person awkward, standoffish, hostile, or lacking in basic social skills?* If so, that might be enough of a reason to skip this new relationship altogether.

The idea here is that the default setting—what most people would expect as a baseline of emotion—varies widely between cultures and personalities. And when we experience a mismatch in positivity and smiles, we can easily misinterpret not only the meaning of those differences, but also what they say about the other person and our desire to get acquainted.

FORMALITY

A second characteristic of presence is formality, which includes two aspects: (a) what is the standard of appropriateness and politeness, and (b) how crucial is it that you uphold that standard to make a good impression? There are quite a few decisions involved here, including how you dress, the kind of language you use, and how much attention you give to the hierarchy. As a simplification, we could say that people from a very formal culture would generally have more exacting expectations about the rules and would assess and judge new acquaintances on their ability to follow them. On the other hand, people in a casual culture might not think the rules matter all that much (or might question the notion of rules to begin with), and accordingly, they also might not be that troubled by people's willingness or ability to abide by them. Now, as with enthusiasm, formality is a product of both your personal style and the culture you were raised in, as well as the culture of your organization or industry. For example, in many countries banking and professional services would likely be more formal than a startup or nonprofit. And each country might have significant regional and generational differences, too.

For now, let's explore what this looks like in different kinds of countries. First, we have Iceland, which is quite informal. Here, it's common in organizational settings to speak freely and informally. People are used to addressing each other by first names—even top executives. And these executives will often share an open office space next to employees, rather than closing themselves off in a private office. The idea here is that they don't need to signal to everyone else that they have a higher status—and they don't depend on employees acknowledging that as a source of respect. Dress is relatively informal as well, though this still varies by industry and company. This isn't to say that people don't care about the impression they make, but instead that they don't expect people's impression to be made largely by their adherence to formality.

By contrast, in other cultures formality sends strong messages about people's caliber and status. For example, our Egyptian colleague said that a director in her country would never drive a used compact sedan to the office—because if they did, none of their staff would take them seriously. After all, if they drove like an entry-level employee, how could employees ever see them as a leader? Similarly, an American finance executive in India was advised that she needed to wear more gold. To this no-nonsense professional, jewelry was an afterthought—and as a woman in a traditionally male-dominated industry, she hesitated to pile on the bling. But her cultural mentors advised her that in India, if she didn't dress the part, she wouldn't be taken seriously. Of course, in Egypt and India, the formality doesn't stop at the parking lot or with one's fashion decisions, but also gets carried into how people speak and act inside the office.

From a global work perspective, neither the Icelandic way nor the Egyptian or Indian way is "correct." Most of our approaches make sense in our own cultures but from 30,000 feet look pretty arbitrary. However, if you assume your way is the right way (that is, if you are projecting), then you are likely to misunderstand and misinterpret your potential colleagues right from the start. You might think they are not nearly serious enough—or too serious. And as a result, you might miss out on a chance to get to know them.

DIRECTNESS

Directness pertains to how straightforwardly people typically communicate in each culture. For example, do people tend to say precisely and succinctly what they mean? Do they get to the point and "cut to the chase"? Or do they hint at what they mean or tell a story, leaving the listener to connect the dots on their own? This is related to a second aspect, which is the interpretation that we give to communication styles. That is, do we see them as efficient, honest, considerate, illogical, and so on? Here again, personality and experience can matter a lot when shaping the directness of any given person's style. However, culture also plays a role in guiding our expectations about what is commonly considered professional and appropriate in the workplace.

For example, Koreans are generally more indirect at work, particularly because they are mindful of group harmony and others' emotional well-being, dignity, and social prestige. But there are different rules according to the hierarchy. While indirectness is especially crucial when interacting up the ladder, Koreans can communicate quite directly and straightforwardly when communicating down the ladder. Peers have more flexibility, but they are still conscious of saving face and the need to demonstrate politeness. But having said this, the younger generation of Koreans working in global business—many of whom received their undergraduate or MBA degrees in places like the United States and Australia—may be far more direct than earlier generations (although still quite respectful and deferential toward authority, relative to workers in Western countries). Finally, things change significantly at night when Korean colleagues go to dinner or for drinks. Away from work, Koreans can behave somewhat more directly—even with superiors.

At the opposite end of the spectrum, we have Germans, who are famously direct with their communication style. They do not typically qualify what they say with expressions like "I might be wrong, but . . . ," "In my view . . . ," or "perhaps we could consider . . . ." Instead, they strive to present their perspective as directly and matter-of-factly as possible. And they take pride in this style because they see directness as precise, honest, clear, and efficient, which are all important German cultural traits. As a result, Germans do not typically soften performance feedback at work, valuing honest, direct communication over soothing or protecting a person's ego.

There are regional variations within countries, too. For example, Melissa had an interesting experience with directness while working in Minnesota as a young adult. As she recalls:

After graduating, I worked in various jobs, including one with a local Midwestern boss who was so indirect that she communicated her expectations and feedback on projects by leaving cryptic Post-it Notes on my desk! This was confusing to me, because I was from a more direct part of the country and had always assumed that it was best to say what you had to say—as politely as possible, but also plainly. I wasn't sure if this meant that I'd done something wrong—was my boss freezing me out by refusing to communicate? To resolve this confusion, I turned to a colleague—someone several decades older, who had been with the organization a long time. She found it amusing and assured me that it wasn't typical in Minnesota for all bosses to do this. But she explained it in terms of a concept called "Minnesota Nice," which refers to the strong cultural desire to avoid conflict. And one way to do this is to be discreet and indirect. This still wasn't my preferred approach to communication—but at least now I could see the logic!

Now, let's imagine what would happen if four people from very different cultural backgrounds were working together on a new project team. One was making ironic remarks that weren't entirely clear but sounded like possible insults. Another discovered they were the youngest (which, in their view, gave them the lowest status), and thus spoke obliquely to everyone to avoid any possible offense. A third said exactly what the problem was, in precise, targeted bullet points. And a fourth tried to be as nice as possible by only addressing issues offline. Each of these people could be perfectly professional with good intentions, yet still misunderstand one another, and in that misunderstanding, struggle to launch a productive relationship.

It's important to remember two key points about all three elements of presence: enthusiasm, formality, and directness. The first, as we've emphasized throughout, is that the origin of a person's style might be cultural, it might be personality or life experience, or it might be a mix of both. And for the purposes of building a relationship, it doesn't necessarily matter where exactly each of their influences comes from.

And second: What matters ultimately is not that person's style *per se*—or even how it differs from yours. What matters is how you make sense of the difference in style—how you perceive it, interpret it, and respond to it. If, for example, your expectation is that a person from a particular culture will be very informal and enthusiastic, but they're not—how do you react? How do you make sense of their behavior? What do you conclude about them? Our hope here is that you will recall our previous discussion of prototypes and treat this discrepancy in your prediction as a point of curiosity and as a preliminary observation—not something totally set in stone. By doing this, you open yourself up to learning more about a person over time without having the embers of a potential relationship be snuffed out by your initial, immediate, instinctual reaction.

A THOUGHT EXERCISE

- Think about your own relationship-building style. How would you characterize your own typical level of enthusiasm, formality, and directness?

- What are you typically looking for when you meet someone else as you determine whether you want to get better acquainted?

- Do you notice that you adjust this style depending on the situation you're in?

LET'S TEST-DRIVE
THE 6 P'S

Now it's your turn to try the 6 P's on for size! You can apply this framework to any case of relationship building to help identify potential areas of overlap as well as diagnose potential areas of misunderstanding. You will likely not find a strong challenge or difference for each element of the model, but even one area of difference can result in uncertainty, misperception, and a potential challenge to relationship building.

Think of a person you are working with who comes from a different cultural background than you do. And remember, this person might be from a different country—but not necessarily. If you recall our earlier discussion of the spice blend, we all have multiple cultural influences (such as region, gender, job function, and so on), not to mention our own personalities. With this in mind, consider the following:

Power

- From your perspective, is it culturally appropriate for you to cultivate a relationship with this person, given any relevant status or hierarchy differences?

- What do you think is the case from their perspective? Although you can't read their mind, what do you know about their culture, and what do their actions tell you?

- Is there a gap between your code and theirs?

- How significant of a challenge does this pose, and what are some ways you can approach this relationship?

Purpose

- What kind of relationship are you seeking in this particular situation? Is it transactional, so that you can get the work done? Is it personal—something that is meaningful for its own sake? Or is it transformational, like a mentor? Perhaps more than one of these?

- What kind of relationship do you think the other person is seeking in this situation?

- Is there a gap between your code and theirs?

- How significant of a challenge does this pose, and what are some ways you can approach this relationship?

Place

- In your view, what is the most appropriate place to cultivate a workplace relationship? For example—is it during the workday, or is it outside of work at events like happy hour? Do you see relationships as being separate from work altogether? Or do you think that work relationships can even be fostered on personal time—for example, at weddings?

- What do you think is the other person's perspective?

- Is there a gap between your code and theirs?

- How significant of a challenge does this pose, and what are some ways you can approach this relationship?

Privacy

- How much information about yourself do you feel comfortable sharing, and how much personal information do you hope the other person will share?

- How do you think they would answer this question?

- Is there a gap between your code and theirs?

- How significant of a challenge does this pose, and what are some ways you can approach this relationship?

Pacing

- How much time do you need to get acquainted with strangers before you can get down to business?

- How much time does it take you to start feeling comfortable and familiar enough with another person that you share personal information with them?

- How long would it take to consider someone a colleague or friend—or is time not a relevant factor for you at all?

- How do you think the other person would answer these questions?

- Is there a gap between your code and theirs?

- How significant of a challenge does this pose, and what are some ways you can approach this relationship?

Presence

- What degree of formality feels right to you? And what degree of formality does the other person seem to prefer?

- How emotionally expressive are you? And how emotionally expressive do they seem to be?

- What degree of directness are you comfortable with? And what degree of directness do they seem to use?

- Is there a gap between your code and theirs?

- How significant of a challenge does this pose, and what are some ways you can approach this relationship?

Take a look at your answers for the 6 P's. Which areas have small or insignificant gaps? Which P's have the greatest gaps and pose the most significant challenges?

———

Now let's look at the 6 P's framework in a real-world situation. This example involves two people—Matthias and Gabriela—who are colleagues on the same global team.

Matthias is from Stockholm. He was raised in Sweden with a Swedish father and an Indonesian mother and sees himself as a global citizen who is equally at home in any culture. Not only does he speak native Swedish and conversational Indonesian as well as business English, but he is just as likely to crave pickled herring as durian (a spiky tropical fruit known for its creamy, mildly sweet taste and its potent aroma)—both acquired tastes for the uninitiated! After a childhood spent between these two countries, he ventured to Denmark for his MBA in global business. He currently works as a senior VP for a Swedish multinational in Stockholm.

Gabriela recently moved to Rio de Janeiro from Manaus, Brazil, and joined Matthias's team as a junior associate. Like Matthias, Gabriela is multilingual and speaks Portuguese, English, and a bit of Spanish. On a steamy day, she is always up for some açaí, but her favorite guilty pleasure is a Portuguese *pastel*, or custard tart. Gabriela didn't have a global childhood, but her study abroad in Portugal ignited a passion for seeing the world—and in fact, that formative experience motivated her to join this Swedish company and build an international business career.

Even though Matthias and Gabriela have completely different cultural backgrounds, they both speak more than one language, have previously jumped at the chance to study in other countries, and have the kind of attitudes that are open to encountering and enjoying new things. So, on the surface, we might assume that they would easily work well together. But before we reach that conclusion, we will first explore their own preferences on the relationship code.

POWER
Who Can You Have a Relationship With?

Matthias has been influenced by two different cultural traditions—Indonesian and Swedish—that have very different orientations toward power (with Sweden being much less hierarchical than Indonesia). When it comes to his professional self, Matthias identifies much more with his Scandinavian side—especially since he attended university in Denmark. So, his default view is that it is perfectly acceptable to have a relationship across the hierarchy, and that either party should feel comfortable initiating and cultivating that.

Gabriela also feels quite comfortable building relationships with anyone at work. She's used to more hierarchy in the office, but not in a highly stratified sense. She likes knowing who is in what role and what their responsibilities are, but that has never stopped her from relating to coworkers on a human level. Her bosses in Brazil took a personal interest in her, almost in a paternalistic way, and she always felt at home as a result.

Bottom line: The role of power in Gabriela's and Matthias's respective relationship codes is not likely to present a major challenge.

PURPOSE
What Is the Goal of This Relationship?

Matthias and Gabriela are mostly aligned here in the sense that the relationship would be a mix of instrumental and personal—and neither is construing it as a mentorship. For Matthias, the instrumental part is the fact that getting to know Gabriela—and others on his remote team—will hopefully make the project management smoother. Gabriela, too, would like to see the project go smoothly—though for her, the main appeal is personal: she'd really like to get to know people on the team more personally in the process of completing tasks. So, their priorities are different—but if we imagine the personal and instrumental as two overlapping circles on a Venn diagram, we can see that both parties can achieve their goals in the process of working together.

Bottom line: The role of purpose in Gabriela's and Matthias's respective relationship codes is not likely to present a major challenge.

PLACE
Where Does Relationship Building Typically Take Place?

Right now, this relationship is being forged virtually, through weekly Zoom meetings and periodic emails and via Slack, where team members frequently post messages about the project. Both Gabriela and Matthias are OK with this—for them, it is just the reality of the dynamic that is baked into this being a globally dispersed team. To Matthias, it also feels efficient because he can manage the project details and also easily give face time to colleagues far away.

Gabriela hopes to meet the rest of the team in person one day, but in the meantime, she is more focused on how to use their virtual tools to create more vibrant connections. For example, she has been thinking about suggesting that they open a channel on Slack for something more fun and personal like photo sharing, so that she can get a better sense for people's personalities and who they are on a human level. However, since she's so new at the company, she hasn't developed the courage yet to give this a shot. She might ask another coworker what they think.

Bottom line: The role of place in Gabriela's and Matthias's respective relationship codes is not likely to present a major challenge.

PRIVACY
How Readily Do People Share Personal Information?

Here is one area where Gabriela and Matthias are *not* aligned—and this difference in style has created some awkward moments in the early stages of their relationship. Gabriela not only feels very comfortable revealing personal information about herself and her family, but comes from a culture where she expects the same from others. As a result, she finds Matthias's style to be somewhat contradictory and confusing: he seems pleasant and nice but also cold and distant at the same time. For example, last week she told a story about her personal life, and he seemed to nod politely without reciprocating. This left Gabriela feeling that he wasn't very interested in her as a person, or that he wanted to remain aloof for some reason. And this planted a seed of doubt about how he perceived her, how she should act, and whether she actually belonged on this team. She thinks, *If her boss isn't interested in having her there, doesn't that signal something to everyone else, too?*

Meanwhile, Matthias wonders why Gabriela seems to ramble during the initial greeting stage of the team's Zoom meetings. He doesn't want to be heavy-handed, so he lets her talk, but he also has his eye on the clock and doesn't want to encourage her to go on longer than a minute or two. It's not that he doesn't care, but he is mindful of everyone's time—and with multiple time zones at play, he wants to make sure the call starts and stops on schedule. Even if he had abundant time, he probably still wouldn't share much about himself. He likes to keep his private life private—it simply doesn't need to be discussed at work. And anyway, there's not that much to share!

Bottom line: The role of privacy in Gabriela's and Matthias's respective relationship codes is likely to present a significant challenge.

PACING
How Quickly Do Relationships Progress?

Gabriela and Matthias seem aligned on how quickly the relationship is progressing. Although Gabriela would like to get to know Matthias better as a person, her concern is about his sharing, not about whether it is taking too long. And although Matthias does not feel a reciprocal need to divulge information about himself, the reason is that he's not a big sharer, not because it is "too soon."

Bottom line: The role of pacing in Gabriela's and Matthias's respective relationship codes is not likely to present a major challenge.

PRESENCE
How Do People Make That First Impression?

Gabriela is definitely *not* formal—quite the opposite. She is very friendly, cheerful, warm, and bubbly, and her wardrobe is full of bright, splashy colors that light up their Zoom calls. Matthias is also quite informal. From his Indonesian upbringing, he appreciates formality and feels natural if that seems to be the expectation in a particular setting—for example, when he does business in Asia. But his own interaction style is quite informal, matching Gabriela's.

On the other hand, enthusiasm is another area of mismatch. From Gabriela's perspective, Matthias is unnervingly stoic and reserved, and she isn't sure what to make of that. At first, she interpreted it as a sign that he was unfriendly or unmotivated to get to know her. But he does seem like a nice guy, and she understands that Swedes don't tend to show a great deal of emotion. For the time being, she's willing to go with the flow—even though she prefers and misses that sense of spontaneous warmth. Secretly, though, she hopes to eventually pry him out of his shell and get to know the real him. For his part, Matthias doesn't necessarily mind that Gabriela is more gregarious than he is—in fact, it is appealing in a way. But he also doesn't know how to channel it into their work, let alone engage with it.

Directness—the third aspect of presence—isn't a mismatch in this case. Gabriela and Matthias are about equally direct. So, neither comes across to the other as too vague or too blunt.

Bottom line: Because of their difference in emotional expressiveness, the role of presence in Gabriela's and Matthias's respective relationship codes is likely to present a significant challenge.

By using the 6 P's framework, we can go beyond surface-level differences like which country each person comes from and become aware of more meaningful areas of overlap, divergence, and nuance in the way each person approaches relationship building on their global team. Although the P's themselves aren't the resolution, they provide Matthias and Gabriela with clarity—and this is valuable, because it shows that the two colleagues have quite a bit in common! There are no major challenges in 4 of the 6 P's (*power, purpose, place,* and *pacing*), which suggests that they are more in sync than not. Moreover, by isolating the specific areas that do seem to pose challenges, they can focus their energy where it is likely to have the biggest impact: *privacy* (what personal details they share, and how much) and *presence* (specifically, how emotionally expressive they are).

As we saw, Matthias is less emotionally expressive, is more reserved, and tends to disclose less personal information. Gabriela is the opposite—and since she also craves a personal relationship, and these differences make it harder for her to attain one, it may mean that she ends up feeling lonely and like something is missing, whereas Matthias likely won't experience the relationship that way at all. Now, these differences in and of themselves won't automatically doom this professional relationship. But they could set a negative spiral in motion if Gabriela interprets Matthias's style as an indication that he's not interested in cultivating a strong professional relationship (or not interested in her, period)—or if Matthias is similarly put off by what he perceives as an overly friendly and familiar demeanor—and then either withdraws from the relationship as a result. However, if you recall our garden metaphor, there are plenty of positive steps that Matthias and Gabriela can take, as we'll explore in the pages ahead.

SECTION 2
BEGINNINGS

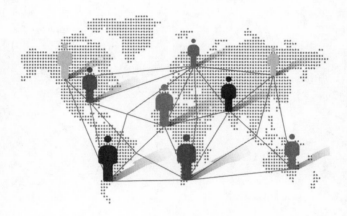

Y ou've boosted your mindset by correcting for biases and used the 6 P's to uncover the implicit or unspoken rules and rhythms for relationship building—keeping in mind that it's not just the country that matters, but other layers of culture (and likely personality as well). Your next step is to discover opportunities to forge that initial connection. In the pages that follow, we detail strategies we learned for doing that from the global professionals we interviewed for this book.

HOW TO START
A CONVERSATION
WITH SOMEONE
YOU DON'T KNOW

You've probably had the experience of meeting someone for the first time and having a gut instinct that they were someone you were interested in getting to know better—or not. Psychologists have studied this phenomenon of what they call "thin slices"—or highly accurate, quick impression forming—since the early 1990s. In fact, one of the main researchers in this area who was profiled in Malcolm Gladwell's book *Blink* was Nalini Ambady, one of Andy's advisors in the PhD program in psychology and organizational behavior at Harvard. This research has been applied to multiple contexts throughout the years. It's a robust, consistent finding that people develop quick and accurate impressions of others in social interactions.[1]

Consider that someone we don't know is like a blank canvas. We know nothing about them and don't really have much of an impression yet. And they know nothing about us and may not have much of an impression of us, either. But then one of us starts a conversation, and very quickly—exceedingly quickly according to the research—the canvas is suddenly painted with colorful brush strokes of our impressions. We may find them interesting or odd; attractive or unattractive; compelling or boring; appropriate or inappropriate. And they form an impression of us, too. The relationship develops—or fails to develop—in large part based on these early impressions.

This presents a challenge when working across cultures, for all the reasons that we have talked about previously. Think about it: if everything you know about how to make a good first impression doesn't align with everything that I assume to be true, then there is a pretty good chance that I'll misinterpret what you are doing. And vice versa—you might also misunderstand my best efforts! But we still need to get to know each other somehow if we are going to establish trust and accomplish shared goals together in our global work. *We need to kick-start our global bonding.* So, the question remains: How do you create a positive first impression?

THE QUASI-UNIVERSAL NATURE OF SMALL TALK

One of the most common types of conversations in global business is what we'll call *small talk*. We recognize that not all cultures or people engage in this casual, informal chitchat about nonserious topics, often as a precursor or "appetizer" to a more professional and structured conversation. If you come from the United States like both Melissa and Andy do, you may assume that small talk is universal—that everyone does it as part of everyday communication. But if you come from, say, Russia, Germany, or South Korea, you might not commonly engage in this form of conversation inside your own cultures at all (although you might, especially if you have had experience living, working, or studying in a culture where this type of communication is more common). And in other cultures, like Jordan's, you might do a form of "long talk"—lengthy conversation that goes far beyond talking about the weather.

Our research into small talk practices in global work has led us to two conclusions. The first is that small talk *is* what you might call "quasi-universal." It certainly doesn't exist everywhere. But in many places around the world, *some form* of a getting-to-know-you conversation exists, especially in international business and studying abroad contexts. (In an upcoming chapter, we will illustrate some of the cultural differences in small talk around the globe.) With that in mind, let's have a look at some common strategies for making small talk—especially when initiating conversations with people you haven't previously met.

YOU HAVE MORE IN COMMON THAN YOU THINK

Many of us are understandably hesitant to reach out and say something to a stranger. However, in a global work setting, you likely have more in common than you realize, and one of the tricks of starting conversations is to notice and take advantage of these similarities. Consider the in-person work event (the kind of situation where you might need to say a few words). One obvious commonality here is that you are both in the same physical space.

For example, imagine you are at a conference in Southeast Asia, and you wander over to the breakfast buffet. There is another person standing there who you are interested in speaking with. Even if you don't feel ready to ask them something personal—or if you are unsure whether they'd be receptive to such an overture—you could still comment on or ask them about something in your immediate vicinity: the food.

You might smile and say, "Good morning" while filling your mug with coffee or tea. And then you could follow up with, "I've never seen this kind of pastry before. What do you think it is?" If the person ignores you or shrugs and walks away, you haven't lost anything because you didn't know them, anyway. But if they sense that you are trying to establish a connection, and they are open to that, they might respond by saying, "Why yes, this is actually a very common Filipino bread called *pandesal*. The purple one is *ube* with cheese—that's really popular these days. And the brown one is traditional."

You still don't know much about the other person—their likes and dislikes, their life story, and so on—but you've nonetheless managed to create a potential spark. You might even decide to extend the conversation with more small talk. For example, you could continue with the bread topic (if you're really into bread or can't think of anything else) by asking, "So, how do you know about *pandesal*?" Or you could shift to something conference-related: "So, what brings you to the conference?" You could even (bravely) ask if they'd like to join you at a nearby table. The exact topic doesn't really matter. The point is that you are interacting in a surface-style way that is safe, relevant, and pleasant—with the possibility of a deeper connection later.

A related approach is to engage the person in a conversation that is about *themselves*—a style that may work better in some cultures than others. Sticking with the conference setting, imagine that you're sitting in a hotel lobby in the vicinity of another conference goer. Perhaps the other person is using a new tablet computer that you also use, or that you'd like to try. Or maybe they have a backpack or briefcase with a sticker on it that catches your eye. These can serve as "props" for initiating a conversation. You might, for example, say, "Is that the new Apple computer? I've had my eye on that. Do you like it?" Or: "Is that a Danish sticker on your backpack? Are you from Denmark?"

In the end, it doesn't really matter if they are from Denmark or own an Apple computer. It's that these are starting points for a conversation—and by starting a conversation, you are showing the other person that you are interested in having one. (Perhaps they are interested, too.) At the same time, you are also gathering information to help you determine whether to continue and extend the conversation.

ASK OPEN-ENDED QUESTIONS

In addition to using the local context to spark a conversation, another tool for initiating small talk discussions is asking open-ended questions. We often don't pay particular attention to the way we phrase the questions we ask. However, small differences in phrasing can have a surprisingly big impact on the way conversations develop. Take, for example, the simple idea of asking a colleague about his trip. There are multiple ways to phrase this opening comment. You could ask the person, "Did you like your trip?" or "Was the trip good?" Or you could also say something like "Tell me about your trip" or "How was the trip?" Do you notice any differences between these two sets of opening comments? With the first two comments—"Did you like the trip?" and "Was the trip good?"—you are basically setting up your colleague to respond with a simple yes or no, which brings the conversation to a halt. For example, the conversation could go something like this:

> **You:** Hi Juan. Did you like your trip?
>
> **Juan:** Yes—it was great. Thanks!

And that's it. The conversation ends—or at the very least it stalls, potentially awkwardly. Then, you must work to reignite it if you are still interested in trying to get to know the person.

A simple trick to encourage a lengthier answer so the person shares more information with you is to rephrase your opening gambit. Instead of saying, "Did you like your trip," try, "How was your trip?" or "Tell me about your trip!" Although you might still get a short response, the chances are now greater that the person will elaborate. The revised conversation might go something like this:

> **You:** Hi Juan. I heard you just got back. Tell me about the trip!
>
> **Juan:** It was great. We went to the Grand Canyon for a few days, and then rented a car to drive to Las Vegas, and then continued down the coast to San Diego. It was our first visit to that part of the US, and my family already wants to go back again. How about you—have you been out there yet?

As you can see, thanks to using open-ended questions and comments, you have learned a great deal more about Juan and his trip, and accessed a range of possibilities for extending the conversation and getting better acquainted. (It was probably also more enjoyable for you, too.)

IT'S NOT THE TOPIC—IT'S HOW YOU DISCUSS IT

People assume that when making small talk, you should stick to neutral, noncontroversial topics and avoid expressing strong opinions so you don't inadvertently offend the other person. This is true, to a point. You certainly do not want to offend them if your goal is to create an opening where you can get to know them in a positive way. However, based on our experience and observations, it's not necessarily the topic you are discussing that matters the most, but how you discuss it.

Take, for example, the very common and "safe" small talk topic of the weather. If you were to observe the hundreds of thousands of small talk conversations that occur every day—at least in the United Kingdom and the United States—the weather would be high on the list of discussion topics. It's something people immediately have in common—and anyway, what could you possibly say about the weather that would be controversial or off-putting? True—but how you talk about it still matters. You can make a comment that is uninteresting yet appropriate, interesting and appropriate, or interesting but completely inappropriate.

Here, for example, is a relatively boring comment you might make about the weather during a small talk conversation: "Did you notice how sunny it is today?" While appropriate and acceptable, this comment is also relatively bland. Although it will certainly spare you from offending other people, it will likely not spark an interesting interaction.

You might not think it would be possible to say something interesting about the weather, but consider these examples: "Can you believe how hot it is? I saw online that some guy tried to fry an egg on the sidewalk!" Or: "This rain reminds me of a few years ago when it rained every day for an entire week! That was before you moved to Seoul, right? I hope you have a good umbrella!" These are not the most interesting remarks imaginable, but they do have a glow of personality—and most important for our purposes, they engage the other person in conversation.

Alongside these boring and interesting possibilities, you could also discuss the weather in a completely inappropriate manner. For example: "Are you looking forward to the storm this weekend? I am because I hope lots of people get flooded basements." This would obviously be bizarre—but it underscores that it's not just the topic itself, but what you do with it that counts.

SHOW YOUR INTEREST
IN HAVING A CONVERSATION

Finally, a last tip for navigating the initial stages of small talk is to show your interest in having a conversation in the first place. In the United States this typically means a relatively enthusiastic style: being positive, upbeat, and friendly even if you don't know the person and have never spoken. It is acceptable and appropriate (even expected) in many situations to communicate in a quite friendly manner, almost as if you were already friends. This signals an interest in making a connection, which, alongside relevant opening comments, is a critical first step toward initiating the small talk interaction that sparks the relationship. And it's not just the United States—an outgoing, animated style is characteristic of many Latin American cultures as well.

In other cultures and contexts, however, this is not at all how you would communicate with a stranger. For example, we spoke to Ryan, an independent filmmaker from Los Angeles who attends major film festivals to network with potential buyers and distributors for various international markets. He explained that at these events, most of his interactions are about as casual as they'd be in Hollywood—in fact, he observed that to a large degree, the overarching "film industry culture" transcended any significant national culture differences. But there was one important exception, which was when he got the opportunity to meet a prestigious Korean director. This moment was highly significant because he had a lot of respect for him and wanted to make a good impression. Moreover, the meeting came thanks to a connection with a Korean colleague, and he anticipated that his actions would reflect on her, too. So, he found out exactly what to do—how to say hello in Korean, how to bow, how to handle the business cards, and so on—and he practiced! Although his delivery likely wasn't flawless, he was able to make a good enough impression to gain access to the professional conversation he sought.

Of course, alongside expressing your own interest, it is also important during these initial stages to gauge the *other person's* interest, too. You might watch their body language and listen carefully to how they respond. Do they seem positive and upbeat? Do they smile and communicate with interest and enthusiasm? Do they provide multiword answers or ask you questions in return? Or do they make minimal eye contact, offer terse answers, look at their phone, or seem to want the small talk to end even before it has begun? Remember: Depending on what you observe, it's worth asking yourself whether you are *really* seeing their level of interest, or if you are simply seeing their cultural code and interpreting it through yours.

SIMPLY SAY HELLO
AND INTRODUCE YOURSELF

There is one final strategy that you might try, especially if you strongly dislike small talk, or sense that the other person won't be receptive to it. You might simply introduce yourself and express your desire to get better acquainted in the future. This can sound awkward or unnatural to American ears, but Melissa has had success using this approach with some European and Asian colleagues. As she explains: "Sometimes I just take the lead and say something like:

> Hi. I'm Melissa. I attended your workshop earlier, and I really enjoyed it. I was hoping to talk with you some more, especially because it touched on my area of expertise as well. I know you're busy at the conference, but perhaps we will run into each other again later, and if not, maybe we can connect on LinkedIn.

It is not exactly a riveting conversation, but it is nonetheless a useful way to plant the seed of a connection that you can cultivate later. It can reduce the pressure to be brilliant in the moment, it lets you "feel out" the other person's conversational style, and it gives you an excuse to follow up afterward. And it works: Melissa is still in touch with some of these global connections.

A THOUGHT EXERCISE

What Kind of Conversationalist Are You?

You just read about starting conversations with people you don't know. For some readers, this might feel exciting, while for others, it might feel tedious, pointless, or overwhelming. That is because there is a wide range of conversational types, whether it's due to our own personalities or our various cultures. Look at Table 10.1 and consider which type best describes you. Then think of a colleague and see if you can guess their style, too.

TABLE 10.1 Five Types of Conversationalists

Type	Explanation
Enthusiastic Conversationalist	You really enjoy engaging in conversation and are likely to get the ball rolling when you are around someone new.
Selective Conversationalist	You enjoy conversing on certain topics, with certain people, and in certain situations.
Neutral Conversationalist	You may participate willingly, or even happily, but you aren't going to take the first step or steer the conversation.
Reluctant Conversationalist	You can converse, but would generally prefer not to.
Avoidant Conversationalist	You do whatever you can to avoid getting pulled into a conversation.

TRANSFORMING SMALL TALK INTO REAL TALK

You've taken the leap and started a conversation. You've remarked on the weather or the commute. You've made a comment about the lack of people at the meeting or the coffee the other person is drinking. The good news is that the conversation has now begun—but so has the challenge. How can you transform this initial chat into a longer interaction that strengthens your connection and perhaps leads to a subsequent conversation or get-together?

FIND COMMON GROUND

The goal of the next phase of a small talk conversation is to find common ground—to deepen and extend the conversation so you go away feeling like the interaction was more than a superficial and forgettable exchange of pleasantries. This is where small talk can evolve into an opportunity to discover what you might have in common. And the way you do this is by hitting on a conversation topic that you both are interested in.

Sometimes, you luck out and the first thing you say ends up being a point of common interest and fuels an extended conversation about that very topic. For example, imagine that you walk over to a new colleague's desk and notice that she has several model airplanes displayed. You ask her if she likes flying, and she mentions that she does and she's working on her pilot's license. You mention that you do, too—you fly as a hobby and you recently joined a flying club—and now you're off to the races.

This is an example where the opening ice-breaking comment or question ends up being the topic for an extended conversation. However, it's just as likely that the initial topic ends up being a conversation appetizer rather than the main dish of the larger conversation. In this case, the search is on for an additional conversation topic. There is no precise formula for making that happen, but there is a series of techniques that can increase the chances that it does.

LISTEN TO CONNECT

Another technique doesn't actually have to do with talking; it has to do with *listening*. Listening carefully can be a great catalyst for moving small talk and your connection forward. When you listen attentively and thoughtfully to another person, it motivates them to engage with you in return. If you're really attuned to them, careful listening can also give you information about what they might be feeling or thinking. And that, too, can be a great way to deepen or extend a conversation. Andy recalls the following example:

> Many years ago, I met a doctoral student at a conference and asked an open-ended question about how she liked her program. She responded that she liked it—but her tone and facial expression suggested otherwise. She had a slight frown, looked away, and sounded ambivalent when she described her studies. At a relevant point in the conversation, I gently commented on my observation—and she confessed that she *did* have mixed feelings. And we then started to talk about those, and the conversation and connection deepened as a result.

In this situation, Andy took a chance and decided to share what he was noticing with his conversational partner. It might not have worked, but in this case, it did—and the key was that he paid close attention in the first place. Although this story took place in the United States, it is useful across other cultures as well. This is because we can become so focused on ourselves when we cross cultures—worrying about saying the wrong thing or making some terrible faux pas—that we forget that one of the best ways to deepen and extend a conversation is to show interest in the *other* person: to listen carefully, ask questions, and show that we care about their responses. People generally like it when they feel listened to and sense that others find them interesting. And the same goes for you. If someone listens carefully to what you say, is curious about your life or opinions or experiences, and really engages you in a conversation, it typically feels nice!

That's the point of small talk when trying to connect across cultures: you want to create a context where ideally both of you can share and exchange some ideas, experiences, and information—of course, not deep, dark secrets or the most personal information, but something "quasi-personal" that the other person feels comfortable sharing and can help you get to know them a bit. *Engagement* is the key to this phase. You want to be personally engaged in the conversation, and you want that to be clear to the other person.

ENDING THE CONVERSATION

Ending small talk across cultures can be tricky. Even though it is just a short conversation, often among strangers or acquaintances, feelings can still be hurt if one person feels that the other has lost interest in the conversation (and by extension, in them). One of our Chinese colleagues, Yi Ming, described the confusion he experienced when networking in the United States:

> Recently I went to a networking event for professionals in my field. I was talking to an American named Kyle, and it seemed like we were really getting to know each other and starting to feel comfortable. I noticed that another person suddenly appeared next to us, and it seemed like they were waiting for something. It turned out that they were waiting for Kyle—and Kyle abruptly turned to this other person and started talking to them instead. I know you don't want to dominate somebody's time while networking in the United States, but in China, you would finish talking to the person you are currently talking to, rather than suddenly prioritizing the new person. So, I didn't know what to do. Was he done with me,

or was I supposed to join in an expanded conversation with an extra participant? I excused myself, but we left at an awkward place. Now if I bumped into him again at a future event, I would feel uncomfortable.

We can see how divergent expectations around wrapping up a conversation led to a perfectly good small talk session ending badly. It wasn't just the difference in style that created an obstacle, but the interpretations about what those differences meant. We have advice for both parties. It might help Yi Ming to work with a cultural coach so he is better prepared to anticipate and respond to conversational patterns at future US networking events. But we might also propose that Kyle expand his repertoire, given that he is in a line of work with global career opportunities. Having more awareness and dexterity would serve him, too.

One general suggestion is to verbally signal your intention to wrap up the conversation, so the other person is aware of it and doesn't have a negative reaction to your abrupt departure such as attributing it to a lack of interest in talking with them. For example:

- "I have to go in a few minutes, but before I go, I'd love to hear . . ."

- "I really enjoyed talking with you. I see someone over there I need to speak with as well—but I hope we can continue soon."

- "I have to go, but I really like your advice about X. I'll keep you in the loop about how it goes . . ."

- "I'm enjoying this conversation, but I notice that it's 9:30 a.m., and we only have until 10 to finish the project."

It's also important to signal your interest in continuing the conversation later (if you are indeed interested). You can do this in several ways. You can indicate your interest indirectly, by saying that you hope to have a chance to continue the conversation "at some point." You might even offer your business card if it feels appropriate to do so. If the other person expresses a very strong interest, you might even schedule (or promise to schedule) a follow-up chat.

Indicating your enjoyment of the conversation does two things. First, it shows the other person that you enjoyed talking with them, which hopefully makes them feel that they enjoyed talking with you. And second, their response to your comment also gives you information about whether they enjoyed the conversation and would appreciate a follow-up. This is a final opportunity to gauge your conversational styles and plant a seed for future interactions. And afterward, it may also help to make a brief note to yourself so that when you do follow up, you'll be able to refer to your small talk session. For example, you might create a new contact for a person named Fabiana where you also note that you met at such and such a conference, during which session; that she gave you some great tips for where to get coffee in Milan; or that it was so refreshing to finally meet another professional in your field who has children; or that you hope they had better weather for the rest of their visit to that city. It doesn't need to be detailed, but when you connect again, it will help you show that you were sincere, and it will feel more natural.

You don't want to come on too strong, however. For example, you don't want to stare at the person or be too enthusiastic in expressing your enjoyment of the conversation. That could turn someone off to you and to the possibility of a future interaction. But a friendly, moderately enthusiastic expression of your enjoyment and interest is often appropriate in many cultures.

CHEAT SHEET

Five Tips for Making Successful Small Talk

Culture obviously influences how we engage in getting-to-know-you conversations, but sometimes when we agonize too much over cultural differences, it can make these conversations seem like obstacle courses when it really just comes down to talking with people. The five tips in Table 11.1 will help you make the most of the moments that appear in front of you.

TABLE 11.1   Five Tips for Successful Small Talk

Small Talk Tip	Explanation	Illustration
1. You have more in common with someone than you think.	If you are in the same physical space as someone else, you always have at least that in common. Use it to your advantage.	Talk about the weather or what someone is carrying or doing as a conversation starter. Or talk about the event you are both at!
2. Ask open-ended questions.	Asking questions is a great small talk tool—but only if you ask open-ended questions that extend the conversation.	Ask: "What do you think of the conference so far?" (open-ended) instead of "Did you go to a session this morning?"

(continued on next page)

TABLE 11.1   Five Tips for Successful Small Talk (*continued*)

Small Talk Tip	Explanation	Illustration
3. Share "semi-personal" information to build rapport.	Sharing about yourself is critical, but remember not to share overly personal information. Also, keep in mind that what is considered personal will vary across cultures.	Talk about your favorite travel destinations or what you love to eat or drink. But don't talk about your weight or finances!
4. You can make small talk about anything—even topics you don't initially find interesting.	Don't just think about the topic itself (like "wine"); find a variation on the topic you find interesting.	You might not be interested in drinking wine, but you might be interested in how people make wine—or store or sell it.
5. Give face-saving rationales for ending the conversation.	The last thing you want to do is sabotage the positive vibe you've worked so hard to create.	"I have to go in a few minutes, unfortunately, but before I go, I'd love to hear a bit more about X."

CULTURAL
DIFFERENCES
IN SMALL TALK

I n the previous pages, we outlined a general approach that can help you more courageously and effectively spark initial connections through conversation in diverse professional settings like teams or conferences. However, we also recognize that there are specific norms and rhythms in different countries. So to better understand cultural nuances in these initial getting-acquainted conversations around the globe, we embarked on a mini research study. Here's a taste of some of the interesting cultural differences that we found by interviewing a panel of five young global professionals.

Anna is a banker. She is originally from Russia and is now working in the United States. She is 29 years old. Jin is a marketing specialist who is studying for a PhD. She is originally from China and is now studying in the United States. She is 30 years old. Seo-yeon is a recent college graduate. She grew up in South Korea and is now living in the United States. She is 23 years old. George is a civil engineer and MBA candidate. He is originally from Namibia and is now studying in the United States. He is 32 years old. Mildred is a marketing and sales specialist and MBA candidate. She is originally from Nicaragua and is now studying in the United States. She is 26 years old. We asked them a series of five questions.

QUESTION 1
Is Small Talk Common in Your Culture?

Anna (Russia): "Small talk can happen at work in Russia but would be unlikely to happen on the street."

Jin (China): "Small talk is not very common in China. It's not usually socially acceptable to just talk to strangers."

Seo-yeon (Korea): "In Korea, small talk is only common among people you have seen at least a few times—for example, neighbors, classmates, or coworkers. Unlike in the US, elevator talk is not common in Korea. When I travel from the US to Korea, if the person on the flight next to me is a Korean, it is rare to make small talk. I feel it is unnecessary to make small talk with a stranger. It feels awkward to me."

George (Namibia): "Small talk is common in Namibia, and it involves asking about the person, how they are doing, their family, work, livestock, and business. . . . Namibians have land in the villages where they raise livestock such as goats, sheep, cattle, chicken, and pigs. And they are very entrepreneurial and often have side hustles to make more money, such as catering, doing hair and nails, and selling commodities."

Mildred (Nicaragua): "Small talk is common in Nicaragua. It is casual, unstructured, and tends to become very personal."

QUESTION 2
Where Does Small Talk Happen in Your Culture?

Anna (Russia): "Small talk can happen at work. For example, you meet one of your colleagues and ask, 'Hi, how are you?,' smile and pass by. This is not typically Russian, but many international companies have come to Russia and brought this tradition. In everyday life, however, people don't typically use small talk with friends and family."

Jin (China): "People do make small talk at work. I find that coworkers can be quite close and hang out even after work with each other."

Seo-yeon (Korea): "Small talk with strangers does not happen much. A café is a place to talk with friends, not with strangers. I do make small talk with neighbors and security guards at my apartment. When I did an internship at a hospital in Korea, I almost made no small talk with doctors, nurses, or researchers there—only with other interns."

George (Namibia): "It is very common and easy to talk to anyone, especially in a social setting. Social settings would include, but not be limited to, bars, churches, conferences, schools, and basically everywhere you cross paths with someone."

Mildred (Nicaragua): "Small talk can happen everywhere. However, it is common to see more instrumental talks at the office or work events when you talk to colleagues or immediate superiors or supervisors."

QUESTION 3
Who Do You Make Small Talk with in Your Culture?

Anna (Russia): "In Russia, you only make small talk with people of your level or lower."

Jin (China): "In China, you are generally not supposed to initiate small talk with people way above you in the hierarchy."

Seo-yeon (Korea): "Making small talk with bosses is very uncommon, and it is even considered rude behavior. If a lower-level person is trying to make small talk to a higher-level person in the company, the higher person will think it is impolite and that the lower person is not serious about his or her work. The only exception is when there is a gathering time after work. After work, it is common to have a gathering dinner and drink and you will hear more small talk there. There is an on/off switch for small talk among coworkers. It is usually 'off' at work and 'on' outside of work."

George (Namibia): "People do small talk with anyone. With friends, the small talk goes on and it is more personal. With strangers, it depends on whether the stranger is someone you want to benefit from investing more time in the conversation. If it is someone you are not going to see again, your conversation does not go that deep."

Mildred (Nicaragua): "In Nicaragua, you can make small talk to anyone. However, depending on the level of confidence, the talk can either be short when you don't trust them or don't know the other person enough or extend and get deeper when you talk to a friend or close person."

QUESTION 4
Who Can You *Never* Make Small Talk with in Your Culture?

Anna (Russia): "You don't make small talk with people of higher status than you are in Russia. Usually, you say hello and pass by with your eyes down toward the floor."

Jin (China): "In China, I don't see people making small talk with people serving you tea in a company or with the CEO. It is more likely to happen with people at your level in the hierarchy."

Seo-yeon (Korea): "Small talk would only happen with people at the same level and who are very familiar with each other. For example, I cannot imagine myself making small talk with the CEO of my company. It is also not common between a professor and students or a boss and lower-level employees."

George (Namibia): Namibia is a very open community-based culture where you can easily communicate with anyone. However, there are levels to organizations. In more modern and corporate settings, it is relatively easy to engage in small talk and befriend your employers, but in typical traditional construction or mining-based industries the employers (Caucasians/Afrikaners) and the employees (Blacks) do not participate in small talk. The employers issue the orders to be carried out. There is no friendship between the parties, and the employees may approach the employers to report on work activities."

Mildred (Nicaragua): "There is no strict rule of who can make small talk to whom. Nevertheless, in a hierarchical organizational setting, small talk usually happens among colleagues or immediate superiors or supervisors. If an employee talks to someone above their supervisors such as directors or CEOs, the supervisor could get mad and may ask the employee what the talk was about. This is because supervisors think that the employee may want to show off or complain about him or the team."

As you can see from this panel of young global professionals, there are some similarities and some differences when it comes to making small talk in different countries and contexts. We think their answers demonstrate that to some extent, there are Western norms of communication that have influenced workplaces around the world. But at the same time, many cultures have two styles—one for local employees who may all come from the same culture, and another for employees who are foreigners or global colleagues. Rather than try to memorize any one culture's norms, we think it makes sense to keep this tension in mind. Especially when working with young professionals, you may very well find that your colleagues and employees have a mixture of multiple styles (like the spice blend we mentioned earlier).

SECTION 3
DEEPENING

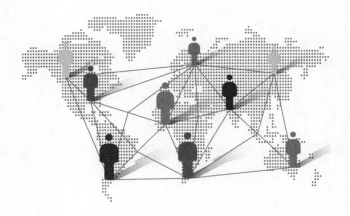

You've made a connection—perhaps you've had a few conversations, know a little bit about each other, and have a sense that this relationship could be something worth growing. You have a feel for your own conversational style, and the style of the person you are getting to know. Maybe you have even noticed some patterns that you think might be specific to their culture. Now, you are ready to deepen, mature, and maintain the relationship. In this case, it's handy to have at your disposal a set of strategies for extending your connection.

LET YOUR
PERSONALITY
SHINE THROUGH

T hus far in the book, we've discussed a series of different
strategies you can use to avoid trip wires and initiate conversations across cultures. What we haven't talked much
about is the internal experience you might have when attempt-
ing to make these connections—in particular, how far you should
step outside your cultural comfort zone to be successful.

One solution is to "go native"—famously expressed by the
adage, "When in Rome, do as the Romans do." It sounds like sensible and culturally sensitive advice, but what happens when the
"Roman way" feels so awkward that it interferes with your ability to engage and interact? Or when there is no obvious "Rome"

to adapt to because everyone on your team comes from a different culture?

In this case, you might consider the opposite solution to "just be yourself." There are significant benefits to "being yourself" when building connections across cultures. The first and most obvious one is that the more authentic and honest you are to begin with, the more authentic and honest the relationship will ultimately be. If you "fake it" and suppress your true nature to adapt, you may be able to act appropriately and avoid faux pas— and thus pass the test that you imagine the cultural encounter to be. But that doesn't mean you will necessarily create a bond and find a connection with someone. After all, if you aren't acting like yourself, then who, exactly, is the other person getting to know?

Being yourself also generally feels better. You feel freer, more alive, less burdened, and more comfortable in your own skin. You don't have to cope with the emotionally taxing experience of suppression—which, as psychological research suggests,[1] doesn't end up working so well anyway, because when we suppress, we don't necessarily do a good job at it. Our emotions can "leak" out into our behavior in subtle ways, and we can come across as awkward, unnatural, and stressed. So, even from the standpoint of appropriateness, suppressing your true nature isn't always the wisest strategy to pursue.

That said, you have probably guessed by now that your authors don't really believe in either-or, black-and-white thinking. And we do think that there also is a time and place for softening or adjusting your instinctive, "authentic" response. After all, you also want to be effective and appropriate—and sometimes "just being yourself" is inconsistent with this objective. Sometimes, you need to adapt to be effective with people who aren't like you.

The key, we've discovered—from our own experiences training, coaching, and working across cultures, as well as from our interviews with experienced professionals—is to recognize that you have a range of different options in your toolkit. At times, you will likely adapt; at other times, you will choose to be yourself; and then in other situations, you will create some sort of blend or fusion between your own style and the style you need to produce in the new setting. This is like a compromise adaptation, where you adapt a little, but not all the way—and in a way that still feels as much like you as possible, or at least that you can live with.

A good illustration of this sort of challenge came from an interview we conducted with a senior American lawyer who was negotiating a big deal with a senior German lawyer from another company. The American lawyer—Amy—was outgoing and provocative. She loved to joke and made small talk very easily. Her German counterpart—Thomas—was the opposite. He didn't make small talk easily or willingly, especially with someone he didn't know. He also prioritized getting down to business instead of chitchatting before a meeting. It was efficient and reasonable, and he didn't feel comfortable being personable with someone this early on.

According to Amy, the first time the two met on Zoom, the conversation was cordial, and Amy consciously chose to tone herself down a bit. For example, she made cursory small talk, but nothing like she was used to. But that changed the next day (at the time, these were daily conversations as the two were negotiating a huge merger on behalf of their organizations). Amy started by asking Thomas how his weekend was. (His answer was "Fine.") Undeterred, Amy asked about the weather in Bonn. (His answer: "Cold and rainy.)

The next day, Amy noticed that there was a new painting on the wall behind Thomas's chair. So, she asked him about it. (His answer: "A gift from my wife.") *Now, we're getting some-*

where, Amy thought to herself. She responded to this opening by saying that she really liked the painting and asked Thomas a few questions about it. The conversation was short, but definitely more personal than before. Gradually, Thomas opened up. Once, during the World Cup, he wore his national German football team jersey. Of course, Amy commented on that, too. The next day, after Germany lost their match, Amy expressed her condolences. Eventually, the deal was completed and the two parted ways. Thomas sent Amy a heartfelt note about their work together—including how much he enjoyed their conversations and camaraderie.

In this scenario, Amy recognized that her default style was going to clash with Thomas's, so she tweaked it slightly. She also cleverly probed and kept an eye out for potential openings— places where she could demonstrate her interest and engage in a positive way. Judging by Thomas's note, her approach yielded results.

So, how do you know how to pick your spots? In our research, we found three key factors to consider: (1) the "strength" of the situation, (2) your relative status in that situation, and (3) time. We look at each of these factors below.

THE "STRENGTH" OF THE SITUATION

Michele Gelfand, a psychologist at the University of Maryland, has researched cultures according to how "tight" or "loose" they are.[2] And we can apply this same concept to situations.

A strong situation is one with very specific, defined rules for how to act appropriately and effectively—and there is little leeway to deviate from these rules. A Japanese tea ceremony would be an example of a very strong situation, because your behavior must follow protocol, with no room for "freestyling." Job interviews are another strong situation. They are not perhaps as tight as a ceremonial ritual, but they do have certain rules and expectations for behavior (that, of course, differ by country, region, profession, industry, and so on). An example of a looser situation would be meeting someone in the break room of an office and having a conversation. There are still certain "rules"—like it would be inappropriate to jump on the table and tap dance—but the "zone of appropriateness" for one's behavior is relatively wide.

The tighter the situation, the more difficult it is to "just be yourself" and the more likely you will tend to veer to the "when in Rome" strategy. Of course, not everyone in these situations will behave in the exact same way, like robots. There will be some variation, but the variation will be much more hemmed in than it would be in a looser situation.

RELATIVE STATUS IN THE SITUATION

The more status you have, the more license you have to be yourself and to experiment with behavior. In Amy's case, the fact that she held equal status to Thomas probably influenced her decision to let her personality shine through. Chances are, if she were much lower status—for example, if Thomas were the CEO of the German company and Amy a lower-level lawyer, she probably would have stuck to the script and accommodated German-style norms. Amy had more freedom to play with her behavior because she had what psychologists call "idiosyncrasy credit"— the license to deviate from social norms.[3] Of course, you can also take chances without these credits—as a very junior person, for example. It's just a bit riskier.

TIME

The third factor is time. All else being equal, you will probably be a bit more accommodating earlier on, as you are planting the first few seeds of trust and connection. Then, as the relationship develops and you become more comfortable with the other person, you can strip away some of that accommodating facade and let more of your own personality shine through. And by the same token, you may also not see your counterpart's full personality at the beginning, either—it may take them time to trust you and open up. If you recall from the example, Amy initially displayed a softer or more muted version of herself, and only after a few meetings did she move to something closer to her fuller self. She was ready to warm up before Thomas was—but then he followed her lead. For some people, that still would have been too fast. They might take even more time to open up. Meanwhile others might feel that accommodating another person for that amount of time is already far too long.

There's no one-size-fits-all approach to being yourself—that would probably be contradictory! But we do want to emphasize that we think it is often possible to let your real self shine through—at least to the extent that you can start to feel natural and less like you are giving a performance. The goal isn't to cloak your real self so that people see what they want to see according to their own cultural expectations. At the same time, we want to remind you that you likely also have a wide range of ways to be yourself that you can experiment with.

14

THE ART OF FINDING COMMON GROUND

Picture the following: It's Monday morning—the beginning of a new workweek—and you hop on a train for your downtown commute. Normally, when you enter a crowded train, you look at your phone, listen to a podcast, or sit there and daydream. After all, what's the alternative? This morning, however, you do something different. Instead of minding your own business, you strike up a conversation—with a stranger. Your goal is to learn something interesting about them and share something about yourself . . . and see how it goes. Does this sound like something you would ever do?

Well, if you were part of the academic study that Nicholas Epley and Juliana Schroeder from the University of Chicago conducted on the train platform in Homewood, Illinois, that's exactly what your instructions would be for the morning.[1] And afterward, you would also complete a survey about your experience and mail it back to them in a stamped, addressed envelope. Epley and Schroeder's goal was to compare what it was like for people to strike up conversations with strangers—to see what they might have in common and to build a connection—when this is the opposite of what they ordinarily would do on their morning commute. They also had a few other conditions in their study—one where people were told to keep to themselves and enjoy the solitude (we probably would have preferred to be in that condition!) and then a "control" condition where they were told to act as they ordinarily would on their commute.

The results of this study and a few others like it were quite interesting. Commuters on the train reported a significantly more positive commute when they found a way to connect with a stranger than when they sat in solitude. This suggests that *connections matter*—even in situations when you might not assume they would, or where it isn't your personal preference. And one of the most powerful ways to build these connections is by finding commonality.

This can be something you have in common in the immediate moment. You are both caught waiting for a bus in a snowstorm. You are both in an office with an amazing art collection. You are both waiting for a meeting to start and everyone else seems to be late. These are examples of things you have in common in the moment. You can also discover through conversation things you have in common at a slightly deeper level. For example, Andy remembers delivering an executive education program for managers at a large Korean company. The session took place in the United States at a university's executive education center. As he recalls:

We finished our morning session and the entire group moved over to the café for a catered lunch. I got my lunch, went looking for a place to sit, and found the only available spot at a table with one other person—who happened to be completely asleep! I remembered him from the morning session, where he was very engaged and asked a lot of good questions. So it was funny and odd that he was sleeping. I sat down very quietly, started eating, and looked at my phone. And then just as I did, he sighed deeply, looked at me, smiled, and told me that he had toddler twins at home in South Korea and this was his first opportunity in a long time to catch up on his sleep. Since I, too, at the time was a new dad, it sparked a conversation about kids and the challenges of balancing work and family. It was an immediate commonality I had with someone who had a completely different cultural background and life story from me.

When you find that you have something in common with someone—whether it's having kids, playing a similar sport, or having a similar hobby—it's an immediate icebreaker. It creates a sense of interpersonal warmth and connection. The other person is no longer a stranger, but someone who feels *just a bit closer* because you can empathize and identify with some aspect of their experience. Also, if you observe interactions where people start finding commonalities, you can see that they might crack a smile, their eyes might brighten, and they might show more excitement in their voice—all signals that they are becoming interested and want to know more. Discovering similarities can thus be a catalyst for kick-starting positive momentum in a relationship.

The global professionals we spoke with had some great tips about finding commonality. A Finnish coach and consultant mentioned that in Finland, where it's not always easy to strike up conversations with strangers, doing so at a particular place or location—like a dog park when you are with your dog or a playground if you have kids—is a great way to increase the odds that you'll have something in common and find that connection. And if you work in Finland—where it can be notoriously hard to get to know one's colleagues—this kind of informal conversation on the side, outside the office, can give you a better sense for how to relate to locals when you do go to work.

Meanwhile, an American CEO who travels overseas multiple times a month shared that he will often cycle through multiple possible topics in a strategy he calls probing. For example, he might start with a person's family, asking about their kids or perhaps even their spouse—though, of course, he understands that in certain cultures, such as Jordan's, for example, these questions would be far too invasive for a first-time meeting. If that feels inappropriate or like a dead end, he'll move on to something else. For example, if it's a culture like the United Kingdom's where weather is a viable topic for small talk, he might go in that direction. And if that's not going anywhere, he might move to asking questions and showing interest in their town or city. The goal here is to ultimately find a match—a topic that engages both parties enough to continue a conversation that feels engaging and authentic. He described it like a treasure hunt, and said that the key is to probe, listen carefully, and then seize the opportunity when you see a potentially fruitful direction.

In addition to common interests, another powerful way to kick-start a potential relationship is to have common experiences. Again, instead of being just a stranger, you are now someone who is a stranger, but with a meaningful point of similarity. These common experiences can be naturally occurring—that is, you don't necessarily do anything to create them. Or they can be engineered. An example of a naturally occurring common experience would be joining an international MBA program where a large percentage of students are, like you, from different countries. You may not necessarily find many people from your own culture in the program, but many people will be in the same boat as non-natives to the country the program is located in.

Another example of a naturally occurring common experience could be going to an international conference abroad. Conferences—especially those that are well organized and provide opportunities to network and socialize—can be great places to kick-start relationships, because in these settings, you typically have at least two things in common: One, you are both interested in the topic of the conference—whatever it may be. And two, you are both also likely not native to the particular city or country where the conference is taking place. This enables you to potentially discover something new together and share common experiences.

You can also create common experiences together with a little bit of intention and planning. Melissa explains how she did this many years ago while working in Phoenix:

> I had a hybrid position, but I made a point to go into the office on days when I knew my coworker was visiting from out of state. I would reach out to her in advance to say that I was looking forward to her visit and I'd like to grab coffee or lunch if she had time in her schedule. These mini get-togethers were an enjoyable way to get better acquainted. And she told me that they meant a lot to her, too—especially because otherwise she would have been left to eat on her own.

In the previous example, we showed how you can make the most of special occasions like colleagues visiting. However, you shouldn't overlook the potential of smaller, everyday gestures. For example, bringing your colleague a coffee back from the café or vending machine is one way to show that you are thinking not only of yourself, but your team. Of course, you'll want to assess for yourself what the dynamic is—there's no reason to go on a spending spree. But in some cultures, this is a fairly easy way to develop a feeling of mutuality and connectedness.

This act of sharing common experiences—especially those that are not virtual and take place in a real-life setting—can be an incredibly powerful catalyst in the process of building relationships because it creates memories. Imagine that a relationship with a colleague begins virtually, but then at some point you find a way to meet in person. You maybe go to a particularly great restaurant (or even one that's comically not so great). Maybe you both have that same experience of the horrible server at the restaurant. And after dining, you both marvel at the amazing street performer right down the block. Or maybe you forget your briefcase or bag and together you have to run back to the restaurant to search for it—and your colleague ultimately finds it. The next week the relationship continues on Zoom. You log into your portal, hit the "join meeting" button, see your colleague's face, and suddenly feel something different than you did before. You feel a bit closer and more connected. You might even laugh about one of the experiences you had—or follow up on something you talked about. This is what we mean by shared experiences— which can be a very powerful tool for sparking and sustaining relationships.

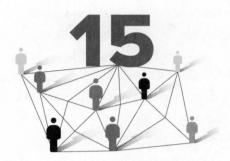

LEARNING THE LOCAL LANGUAGE OF TRUST

When Dawn Pratt finally decided to take the job up in Montreal—far from her Dallas, Texas, home—she admittedly knew very little about Canadian culture. She definitely knew about the Montreal Canadiens, since they were the rivals of her beloved hockey team, the Dallas Stars. She also had once tried poutine—the quintessential Quebecois dish with french fries, cheese curds, and gravy. It wasn't bad, she thought—kind of like a Canadian version of nachos. Oh—and there was one more thing she knew—which wasn't going to help her much since she didn't speak it at all—Canadians in Montreal spoke *French*.

At first, Dawn assumed that French was a secondary language. But as she learned more from reading online, speaking with a few people, and watching YouTube videos about language laws in Quebec, she realized that *français* wasn't just the official language—it was a deeply meaningful and important part of the local culture, too. Fortunately for Dawn, she would be able to conduct her daily work in English because the company was bilingual—but if she stuck only to English, she would be sending strong signals that she didn't respect their local culture.

So, she'd have to at least attempt to use French. And as it turned out, Dawn got this chance during her very first week on the job, when she was tapped as the new head of HR to make a major announcement to the company—which would also figure as part of her introduction to the team. From her previous experience, Dawn knew this was a big deal—she needed to create a positive impression—and this was her first and maybe only chance to do it.

When the day came, she took a deep breath, said a quick silent prayer, stepped up to the microphone, and began to speak very slowly and deliberately:

"*Bonjour,*" Dawn started, with a quiver in her voice. "*Je m'appelle Dawn et je suis de Texas.*" She paused to collect herself and look at her notes. "*Je suis si heureuse de vous rencontrer.*" When she nervously gazed out at the audience, she found a roomful of smiling faces. A few people even started applauding. As Dawn explained during her interview: "These two or three French sentences with my awful Texas accent bought me 10 years of goodwill and an immediate sense of trust." The reason? Dawn had tapped into the local trust language.

Trust is obviously an essential element of relationship building. In fact, it might be the only universal aspect of relationship building that we discovered in our interviews with professionals around the world. In every country, in every profession, and in every relationship-building situation, trust was the glue that held the relationship together and enabled it to grow. But interestingly, although the importance of trust is universal, the way to develop it is very culture and situation specific.

In certain places, *politeness, deference, and respect* are essential to unlocking trust. This was certainly the case for American-born Samit Shah during a key trip he took to Japan hoping to win the business of a large Japanese conglomerate. The company had solicited a series of bids from top global consulting outfits including McKinsey, BCG, and Bain, as well as Samit's boutique firm from Washington, DC. Samit was a thought leader in his industry, and so despite the small size of his firm, he had the potential to compete with these large global players—assuming that he could win the trust of the top Japanese management team.

Samit had been to Japan before but was no expert on the culture, so he consulted with a few knowledgeable friends and colleagues to find out what the key to winning trust might be in this context. As it turned out, the *trust currency* in Japan was to be humble, polite, and formal, but also show confidence. His advisors cautioned that too much humility and politeness would not let him stand out from the pack and highlight his added value. But too much confidence would be disrespectful in front of his very senior Japanese counterparts.

On the big day, Samit walked into the room, ready to deliver his pitch, and was introduced by his main contact at the firm—a more junior person who was perfectly bilingual in Japanese and English. "Samit looks young," the translator said, "but is an extremely accomplished, world-renown expert . . ." Samit's ego started to swell—he liked the sound of that! But he also knew that this was a potential trap. He was being set up to act like the demonstrated expert, but he remembered that to earn trust, he had to behave modestly.

So, when the translator finished, Samit thanked him very politely for such an undeserved but wonderful introduction. And even though he had a very informal rapport with this translator in the moments before the meeting, Samit now used honorific language as a sign of politeness and respect—both for the translator and as a signal for the decision makers in the room.

Samit continued, "You build me up, and I am very grateful for your kind introduction. I don't want to say you're wrong—I do think I have some insights and a background that could be helpful to you—but I want to emphasize that it is *I* who am honored to be here in your company." Samit also spoke slowly enough that the simultaneous translator could do his job in a way that made the overall communication flow smoothly. But the key here was Samit tapping into the local trust language and adjusting his sales pitch accordingly. And it worked: Samit ended up winning the contract and enjoyed an enduring relationship with the company.

It's important to emphasize two things about this story that are relevant to other examples of earning trust across cultures. The first is that for Samit, acting politely in this particular situation wasn't necessarily inauthentic for him. Of course, it was different from how he might have pitched himself and built a relationship in another context or culture—but polite, deferential behavior was something already in his repertoire, albeit more with his Indian relatives than in a business context in the United States. Still, it was there—to use another metaphor, it was on a hanger in his behavioral closet. The second point to emphasize here is that once initial trust is earned, the relationship—and your behavior in the relationship—can and does change over time. Samit didn't remain this formal, polite, and careful with his colleagues forever. On the contrary, he gradually developed a very natural, close connection with them, and it even got to the point where he could safely joke and truly be himself. But to earn the right to build and develop the relationship in the first place, he had to use the right currency of trust at the outset.

We heard so many stories of people working hard to earn trust currency early on in a cross-cultural professional relationship. For example:

- An American consultant in Oxford working with very posh, upper-crust, highly educated Oxford University graduates learned that to earn their trust early on, he had to adopt a somewhat cynical, blasé, detached air. At the same time, he had to be self-deprecating, as making fun of yourself in an artful way was also a culturally valued characteristic in that class-based cultural setting.

- A French consultant in Finland learned that the way to earn trust wasn't necessarily by adopting a particular style or language; rather, it was through being consistently dependable, honest, and professional over a long period of time. This eventually earned her the right to develop a more personal connection with her colleagues.

- An American executive in Quebec City (who hadn't ice-skated since childhood and didn't speak a lick of French) got up early to play hockey with his work team at 7 a.m. He also learned some basic French to honor his teammates and earn their trust.

- A German manager in the United States learned that his American subordinates needed to feel appreciated by receiving praise for good work—even if in Germany, this might be considered simply a regular part of one's job and not necessarily worthy of praise.

What is critical here and what makes the trust language so important is not the specific action itself, but the meta message that it sends to the other person. And that meta message is ideally some version of the following (at least one of these and sometimes more than one):

1. I respect your culture even if it's not my own.

2. I am willing to meet you halfway.

3. I'm someone you can relate to.

4. I'm someone you can count on to do the right thing.

There is one final important point about trust languages that we want to mention. In some situations, acting in a certain culturally preferred way is nice, but flexible and even optional. For example, in the case of the American learning to play hockey and speak a bit of French, you can probably imagine other pathways toward achieving trust that the executive could have pursued if he had no athletic prowess and struggled mightily with foreign languages.

In other situations, however, the language of trust is a "need to do" rather than a "nice to do," and failing to adapt could imperil the relationship (and in the case of a short-term situation, the deal or negotiation). Drinking alcohol is one such *trust gauntlet*, especially in the early stages of a relationship when you are offered a drink by your host, and they expect you to partake in a well-established trust-building ritual.

Indeed, drinking alcohol is a classic way of building global bonds, even at the highest levels of global diplomacy. US President Richard Nixon famously used a toasting ritual during his 1972 visit to China, when he and Premier Chou En-lai toasted each other with small cups of *moutai*. In 1996, US President Bill Clinton raised a pint of Guinness with Irish Taoiseach (Prime

Minister) John Bruton during a visit to Dublin. In 2008, UK Prime Minister Gordon Brown toasted Russian President Dmitry Medvedev with vodka during a meeting in Moscow. And in 2010, US President Barack Obama and Mexican President Felipe Calderón toasted each other with tequila during a meeting in Mexico City.

Imagine if in any of these cases, one of the world leaders had declined the drink. It probably would not have sunk the relationship—but it still could have been unexpected and awkward. Similarly, because sharing alcohol is a long-standing, deeply engrained trust language in many cultures, those who do not drink should think through their response in advance—and recognize that they will need to find other ways of establishing trust that don't compromise their values and health. At the same time, those who come from cultures that emphasize alcohol should likewise anticipate that not everyone they work with will feel the same way—and they, too, should be prepared to have a multimodal approach to trust building in different contexts.

16

MULTIPLE METHODS FOR DEEPENING YOUR CONNECTION

f you think about the relationships in your life, chances are the most meaningful ones are those where you connect across multiple modalities. You might use Instagram or Facebook to share photos; you might text or message via WhatsApp; you might FaceTime each other; and you might also see them in person. For example, you might text a friend or family member the details for a party, attend it together, create an Instagram story about it, and then tag or direct message them to make sure they see it. Or if they couldn't join in person, perhaps you might FaceTime from the event so it almost feels like they are there, too. These modalities reinforce each other—and your friends and family likely use them to respond in kind.

The same holds true for work as well. Think about a colleague you have gotten to know versus someone who is just hovering in your network. If you have only connected or messaged them on LinkedIn and that's it, it's likely they are a peripheral connection and not deeply meaningful and integral to your professional life. But if this is a team member on your virtual team that you've emailed or messaged multiple times; that you Zoom with; that you see at the rare in-person event; and that you also share funny comments with on Slack, chances are this is someone you feel relatively close to and that you have a potentially strong professional relationship with.

The trick then is to recognize the multiple modalities at your disposal and use them strategically. Here are some examples you could use when traveling or when working virtually.

WHEN TRAVELING

Traveling allows many opportunities to form deeper connections by enriching in-person meetings, making room for relaxed small talk, and even sharing appropriate gifts.

ENHANCE THE IN-PERSON MEETING EXPERIENCE

Damar James often traveled for work. When his friends and family asked him how Paris, Hong Kong, or Buenos Aires was, he'd joke, "The Radisson was lovely." He could be in the most enchanting city in the world but would only experience the generic hotel atmosphere—so most of his encounters were bland. One day, however, Damar's boss gave him a simple piece of advice that transformed his experience of foreign travel. His boss suggested that instead of just hanging out in the hotel, getting caught up on email, tweaking his slide deck, or taking a nap, Damar should prioritize exploring the city—seeing a few sights, finding a cool place to have dinner, and experiencing the culture—even if this meant arriving a day early.

The goal of this change wasn't just to make Damar's life more colorful—which it did—and to cost the company a bit more money—which it also did. The real goal was for Damar to have some interesting firsthand experiences inside the local culture that he could share with his counterparts in his meetings the next day. And this worked tremendously well.

Damar started sprinkling into the conversation a few of the things he did. He would also ask questions—ones that were informed and worthwhile because they were grounded in his own exploration. For example, he might tell his counterpart about an inviting little nook of the city he had discovered and ask about something particular he had noticed there. These more nuanced observations and questions were not only conversation starters; they also showed sincere interest, appreciation, and effort in learning about the local culture—which impressed the people he was working with and was a catalyst for deepening the connection.

And this isn't something that only applies to the people who are doing the traveling. The people on the receiving end—those who are in the locations where colleagues and potential clients are visiting—can also do a lot to make the most of their in-person time.

The options on how to do that are almost infinite. One instance we heard about involved two coworkers who decided to see a Lady Gaga concert together. They already knew that they shared a love of her music, and when it turned out that she was performing in the same city that one of them was traveling to for a meeting with the other one—well, they couldn't resist! Now, of course, every employee isn't going to have the same taste in music—and in this case, it was a private choice to attend, not a company-sanctioned and paid-for event. But it was still clear that the act of celebrating a shared interest by singing along together to the same songs elevated their connection to the next level, long after one of them had flown back home.

Tiffany, the director of a global program based in San Diego, is a *maestro* at creating meaningful in-person experiences with out-of-town clients and colleagues. One of her strategies is to always have a capstone event at the end of a meeting featuring local food and drink that spotlights her Southern California culture. For example, she might make dinner reservations at a location where she knows they can enjoy fresh seafood and watch the sunset—maybe aboard one of the dinner cruise ships that sail across the bay. And not only does she craft a shared moment that they can remember, but she takes a picture of the group that's gathered and sends the photo to each person later with their names, the company logo, and a message about how nice it was to spend that time together. She told us that when she visits these same people at their own offices—say, in Mexico and Lebanon—she has seen those very pictures on their desks! They have also told her personally how much these mean to them, and that they cherish the memories of their time in San Diego. Clearly, they haven't forgotten her.

MIX UP YOUR IDEAS OF WHEN TO MAKE SMALL TALK

In the United States, casual conversation often happens spontaneously or in moments that are adjacent to meetings, like chatting quietly beforehand. And sometimes, meetings themselves open with a brief chat. Yet this isn't the only way it can happen. Melissa has heard from professionals in other parts of the world that they are more comfortable focusing on business first, and then using any remaining time in the meeting for conversation. They explained to her that this puts them at ease, because they can focus on their colleagues instead of the task at hand, and it feels like a "treat" for getting the work out of the way. Now, many Americans would see it differently—but *different* doesn't mean *wrong*. If you find that the people on your team aren't loosening up and talking, and this kind of relationship building is important to you, you might try designating a different time—like the end of the meeting—for brief chats.

SHARE APPROPRIATE GIFTS

Another way to establish and rekindle a connection across many cultures is through gifts. Now, gifts can certainly be tricky territory, since there are some gifts that might be considered taboo or inappropriate in certain cultures (like giving knives in Korea). Moreover, what looks like a nice professional gesture from one perspective might appear like a bribe elsewhere. For this reason, many companies have—or should have—clear guidelines about what their own policies are, especially when working with cultures that may have a different interpretation. But the fact that it can be tricky doesn't mean you should avoid it entirely, because just like in a romantic relationship, a gift is an important gesture or overture in a business one. It says, "I thought of you, I value our connection, and I hope that when you look at this item, you'll think of me, too."

Tiffany from San Diego has a great example of how to do this, too. She finds local creators who make San Diego–themed gifts that are distinctive, not tourist-tacky, and within her moderate budget. One of these is a candle that smells like surfboard wax—something that is very San Diegan, although surfing is not unique to that city. This gift is small and sturdy, unlikely to cause offense or be taken out of context, and a tangible reminder of her organization.

But it also serves another purpose: she uses it as a conversation starter! For example, she might say something obvious like, "We hope you'll enjoy this piece of San Diego culture" (or even— "this aroma of California!"). But she can go even further and ask them if they know what surfboard wax is, if they have ever been surfing, if they would like to go surfing sometime, if they have ever seen someone surfing, what they think about surfing, and so on. And then it becomes a conversation starter—which, as you recall from our small talk section, is one way that you can foster your connection. And by cleverly selecting a gift that reflects the culture, she is simultaneously making a nice gesture, reminding them of their connection to her, teaching them about her culture, and getting to know them better. It's a big win!

Gifts don't always have to be in-the-moment to have an impact, either. For example, Melissa met a Polish colleague at a 2014 conference in Portland, Oregon—and then ran into that same colleague again when she attended a 2016 conference in Wrocław, Poland. They reconnected and got caught up—and subsequently, after Melissa returned home, she received a surprise package in the mail. It was a mug set painted with a Polish folk motif. Of course, Melissa enjoyed the functionality of the mug—it was great for drinking her morning coffee. But the key is that every time she used it, the design reminded her of Poland and her contact there. It was the thought that counted—and it was a gift that kept on giving.

WHEN WORKING VIRTUALLY

Working virtually can also give opportunities to forge deeper bonds through techniques such as creating a regular space for sharing, leveraging asynchronous platforms to promote engagement and connectivity, personalizing technology to help team members get to know each other and build rapport, and even establishing group rituals to create a meaningful meeting experience.

CREATE A REGULAR SPACE FOR SHARING

When you work together virtually, you don't necessarily have any intuitive guess about what the other person's life is like. And depending on your personality, that might be fine with you. But if your goal is to work well together—to forge a bond that helps you succeed—then you'll want to be intentional about making space for talking about your individual lives. One way this can happen is in regular weekly or biweekly meetings—whatever your routine is. And it doesn't have to take a long time.

Tom, an executive from Seattle, told us that he would make a point to ask his French colleagues in Toulouse what their plans were for the weekend and what they had going on. His French colleagues would ask about the American side, too. Often, the information shared was trivial, but like confetti falling on the ground, it gradually accumulated to the point that everyone on the call developed a more well-rounded sense for who each other was. The knowledge that Pierre was taking his two children to Switzerland for their spring holidays, for instance, transformed him from Pierre, the generic French coworker, to Pierre, a father who enjoys skiing. In the process of learning about him, he became more human, three-dimensional, and relatable.

This is critical on a relationship-building level because most people don't want to start with details that are very sensitive and vulnerable. If you consistently create a space where people can share what they wish, however, they will often do so—and as that happens, there will be an increased sense of knowing each other. But it's more than that. It can also be a prelude to sharing more consequential information—for instance, that a project is behind schedule, or that there is a misunderstanding of the scope or requirements or some other issue. If you have already invested in building a productive relationship, it will be much easier to then, from the safety of that relationship, address issues that arise. For some readers, this may be obvious—while for others it may seem like a counterintuitive way to think about what work is. But we assure you that even if you come from a culture, or are in an industry, where work is really all about accomplishing the tasks, forging these bonds will still be useful.

Consider this example from a senior project manager named Jeff who was working with multiple team members based in the United States, the Netherlands, France, Malaysia, India, and China. One interesting feature of this project is that the people he worked with didn't report to him—he wasn't their manager. They were all team leaders from their respective units with approximately equal seniority, and the purpose of this specific team was to serve as a coordination point where leaders of each team could collaborate and iron out any kinks to better serve the company.

In this environment, it turned out that forging relationships through weekly phone calls meant that Jeff had a very important heads-up on holiday and vacation schedules—which in some countries also meant that factories would be shut down on the production side of their company. Since some of these holidays such as Ramadan and Lunar New Year didn't have a fixed date on his own calendar and weren't necessarily front-and-center in his mind, he found it very valuable to get these personal reminders so that his team wasn't caught off guard.

Just as significant, these weekly check-ins served as a kind of incubator from which a sense of collective identity as team members ultimately emerged. There was sometimes conflict and disagreement, but because they met every week, it was easier to give each other the benefit of the doubt when a challenge arose. The broader American team might think "that's so typical of India" and vice versa, but Jeff and his counterparts on the Indian team could easily intervene and say something like, "You know, I just talked to Lakshmi on the Indian side, and I think the story is a bit different. I'll talk to her again and see what we can work out." Jeff emphasized to us that these relationships turned out to be a precondition for the internal negotiating and problem solving that took place, because they fostered the trust, mutuality, and sense of safety that was required for the parties to come together. In pretty straightforward terms, he summed it up like this: "Without the relationships, we couldn't have gotten much of our work done."

LEVERAGE ASYNCHRONOUS PLATFORMS

Interactive asynchronous platforms like Facebook, Instagram, Teams, and Slack offer an additional route toward relationship building. These are places where—on your own schedule and on your own time—you can enjoy what other people post and also post content of your own. And the fact that this is communal and reciprocal—you post something and then I post something in return—ends up helping to weave the social threads of our interactions together.

We have firsthand experience using this strategy with the Global Dexterity Certification that we run together with our

Polish colleague, Kinga Białek. The course is a virtual program in which we meet twice a month via Zoom to train coaches, trainers, teachers, consultants, and many others to use the Global Dexterity method (based on Andy's previous book) in their line of work. In addition to being educational, the program has been a fun opportunity to connect with smart and fascinating people around the world. There was only one downside: we worked hard to build this little community and derived a lot of satisfaction from being part of it—but each time, once the cohort ended, our sense of community ended, too—quite abruptly.

Our solution was to create an alumni workspace on Slack where participants from all the previous cohorts could network with each other, announce their professional accomplishments, ask questions about course concepts or how to apply them in a training, and share articles and other resources like books and movies about culture and global work, which is the topical interest that we all have in common. But while those were all important, they were mostly informational and one-directional, and didn't necessarily help us cultivate a sense of mutuality and belonging. So, we added a new channel and illustriously labeled it "Photos-Fun-Food-and-Other Things." We had no clue what to expect—it was just something to try—but the results were amazing.

Here are a few examples:

- A Polish alum posted a photo journal of his trip to the rural Midwestern United States, along with photos of bison and descriptions of his experiences at small town diners.

- A French alum posted photos from her favorite museum exhibits in Paris.

- Several people posted photos of their holiday meals—Thanksgiving in the United States, Christmas in London, New Year's in Jordan, Easter in Russia.

- A German alum even told us how he had attended an orchestra concert in the most unusual location: a drained indoor swimming pool!

As interesting as these insights were, what was most meaningful was the engagement itself—the act of sharing, responding, and observing that pattern. In truth, not everyone posts: some people are prolific, some post periodically, and some never do. But what we've found is that creating a virtual garden or playground where people can freely engage allows people to show up and interact in whatever way makes sense for them at the time. It helps create a feeling of connectedness, warmth, and continuity for the group. And as a sign of how powerful this is, even people who never post have messaged us separately to say they enjoy looking at the photos and getting this glimpse into the daily lives of people around the world.

Of course, there is also the chance that what you share can backfire, so it might be important to agree on ground rules as a team, and to have someone take on the role of moderator—especially if people in your group come from very different cultures without a shared sense of what is appropriate. For example, in one intercultural team that Melissa is familiar with, a misunderstanding ensued when one person posted a photo of himself hunting on a team Slack channel. In the community he comes from, this is a seasonal pastime that is widely participated in across generations, so he never considered that other people might find it objectionable. He was genuinely trying to share about his hobbies—as he had been invited to do—so he could get to know the team better. Unfortunately, there were people from other cultures on the team who found this hobby very distasteful. In response, the hunter took the photo down, but because sharing about himself had opened him to criticism, he simply stopped sharing. And because engaging in the team channel had exposed the others to material that they didn't care to see, they also began to disengage. As a result, not only was the opportunity lost, but in some ways, it ended up worse than if they hadn't used the team channel at all. So, while we do recommend using sites like Slack, it's important to remember that intercultural teams may need a more explicit set of guidelines. You might also consider acknowledging up front that misunderstandings sometimes occur when we connect across cultures—but also that if they arise, they can be mutually addressed and resolved.

One final tip: If you are the manager trying to cultivate this kind of asynchronous space, it pays to think about your own engagement, too. While you may be hesitant to talk about yourself too much, you don't want to be conspicuously absent, either. Thinking back to our scenario with Gabriela and Matthias (the Brazilian and Swedish colleagues who had very different approaches to sharing personal information), Matthias might, for example, post a photo of his dog, a meal, a city skyline, or even the weather if it feels uncomfortable to talk about his family or personal life. And you'll want to think about responding as evenly as possible, too. If you always give a positive response to posts by one person but ignore those by others, it might plant seeds of doubt in the team's mind about how inclusive and welcoming the space really is. In other words, think of your role as promoting engagement and connectivity, rather than just what personally interests you.

PERSONALIZE TECHNOLOGY

When Andy got the memo at Brandeis University that all Spring 2020 classes would be going online, it wasn't surprising. Covid-19 was rampaging across the world, and everything was suddenly shutting down. Universities could still operate, but due to an incomplete understanding of the disease and the lack of vaccines at the time, caution was the order of the day.

As Andy recalls:

We were going online, but the problem was that few of us had ever used Zoom, let alone taught with it. And so our minds were racing with questions: How were we going to deliver the content we needed to? (That didn't end up being much of a challenge.) How could we have students do small-group work in the classes that demanded it? (This also ended up not being a problem, thanks to the breakout room feature.) But the biggest question that gnawed at me was *how could we build relationships with our students and make the class feel truly connected?* That part wasn't obvious. There wasn't an easy tech solution. And we didn't get any particular guidance about how to do that—despite the fact that, at least for me, that was one of the absolute most important parts of teaching.

I decided, along with my teaching assistant Teresa Campos, to try an experiment. We asked each person in the 40-person class (a large percentage of whom were international students) to create what we called a "personal PowerPoint presentation." The presentation was, of course, virtual—and it was meant to be about 3–5 minutes long. In the presentation they were encouraged to introduce themselves to the class any way they'd like. To be honest, Teresa and I had no idea if this would work—we had never tried it before. But it ended up being a big hit. The presentations were great. They were all different, but highly personal. One student from China showed us, through photos and commentary, a day in his life in his small hometown. He showed us where he lived, where he would walk to the fish market to buy fish, and the kinds of dishes his mom would prepare. Others showed images of their high schools from around the world, their families, their pets, and their traditions. Initially, I had feared that I wouldn't be able to get to know my students in this novel online format. But with this little tweak to the syllabus, I ended up feeling more connected to my students and the class as a whole than I ever did in person!

Thankfully, Covid-19 is now a more manageable disease, but we can take what we learned from the experience and use strategies like these to build rapport with a remote group. And one of the lessons is that being intentional pays off. In this situation, the students—who we could easily reframe as global team members for a business context—didn't spontaneously show up one day with mini-presentations prepared about themselves! It was Andy's role as the leader to come up with the idea, explain the parameters, and then carve out time for the activity to take place. He also set the tone during the presentations to make sure that people felt like their participation was welcomed, appreciated, supported, and valued. It did take some work, but not an extraordinary amount. And as you can see, it didn't require any special, expert-level insights into any particular culture's nuances.

CREATE A MEANINGFUL MEETING EXPERIENCE

You probably don't necessarily think of putting together the words "meaningful" and "meeting." After all, a recent survey from the University of North Carolina found that 71 percent of the senior managers they surveyed found meetings unproductive, 65 percent said that meetings keep them from completing their own work, and 62 percent said that meetings miss opportunities to bring their team closer together.[1] Not a great endorsement of meetings, to say the least.

That's why Andy was surprised by how much he enjoyed participating in a meeting a few years ago that was run by the International Academy of Mediators, a nonprofit group of 200 elite mediators from around the world. The group had contacted him to help them brainstorm how to do peacemaking work in a virtual world—and specifically, how to create the quick sense of trust between parties that was necessary for mediation to work. As part of the engagement, Andy agreed to attend one of their monthly virtual meetings, which he found quite interesting. Toward the end, as Andy was getting ready to log off, the person running the meeting announced that it was time for the "monthly toast." As it turns out, each month, one person gave a personal toast—a heartfelt reflection about something on their mind that they wanted to share with the group. And at the very end, that person would raise a glass—alongside all the virtual partici-pants—and have a synchronized sip. For Andy, this was one of the most powerful Zoom moments he had ever experienced. It was sincere, personal, and funny—and the fact that someone dif-ferent delivered it each time kept the tradition fresh.

As it turns out, we were so inspired by Andy's experience that we incorporated this ritual into a monthly meetup that our

Global Dexterity team rolled out during the early days of the pandemic. This free session was an opportunity for people in the intercultural community around the world to network and discuss a topic of the month. Before each meeting, we would invite one of the 40 or so regular participants to offer a toast at the end—just as Andy had experienced with the international mediators. In keeping with the global composition of the group, the toaster was from a different culture each time, and their toast might reflect a particular tradition, or they might teach us something about their culture, or they might give part of the toast in the language of their culture. And just like with the mediators, at the end of the toast, everyone would raise a virtual glass, toast (in their own language), and end the call. It was a great way to create a touch of meaning within a medium (virtual calls) that people had gotten a bit sick of. And since it was repeated each time, it became a ritual that people could expect, count on, and participate in. But the key is that while we made a point to be inclusive and welcoming, it wasn't forced or phony.

SECTION 4

FINER POINTS OF GLOBAL BONDING

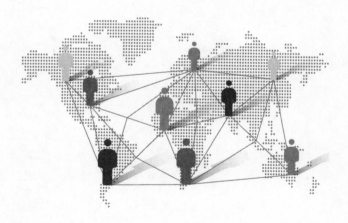

Y ou've mastered the basics of global bonding. You know about the ways that our minds can trick us into making faulty assessments of others and how these biases and

139

heuristics can interfere with relationship building. You've learned about the 6 P's—power, purpose, place, pacing, privacy, and presence—and how gaps between your own style and the other person's can cause troublesome misunderstandings. Finally, you've learned a series of strategies—conversational techniques, ways of building common ground and trust—that can beat bias, foster connection, and strengthen relationships. As you continue to hone your abilities, you will undoubtedly encounter additional challenges along the way, and that's the focus of this next section of the book: helping you stretch your global bonding skills and perfect your craft.

BUILDING RELATIONSHIPS IN A TEAM CONTEXT

s Nalini Doshi pressed *send* on her last email of the day, closed her computer, and looked at the nearly empty refrigerator for something she could possibly eat, she felt demoralized. She had been so excited earlier in the year when her boss had asked her to lead the team in charge of a key product launch. It was her first high-profile opportunity at the firm and her first experience managing a global team. Her initial assumption was that the details of the product launch—the strategy, financing, marketing, and so on—would be the trickiest part. But the reality was that all of this was a piece of cake compared to managing the people dynamics. To be honest, it was a nightmare, and Nalini was very close to quitting her job and abandoning her dream of becoming a top executive before her fortieth birthday. *What had she gotten herself into?*

The biggest problem was the dysfunction between two key IT teams: one in Mumbai and one in Warsaw. Both spoke excellent English, so that wasn't the problem. The issue was *cultural*. For example, the Polish team had a straightforward, direct communication style. They would ask questions like, "Can you deliver this on Friday?," "Do you understand what is needed to be done?," or "Is everything clear to you?" The Indian team would typically answer yes . . . but then not do what was expected. When a deadline wasn't going to be met, the Indian style was to hint at this indirectly: "The deadline is tomorrow, right?," or "The deadline is ambitious," or "Other people have been given additional time to complete this task." The Poles found these responses perplexing. They didn't understand that in Indian culture, saying no directly can be offensive, so communication is often between the lines. But even if they *had* understood it, they still might have rejected it because it didn't fit their standards for professional communication.

From the Indian perspective, things weren't much better. They resented how the Polish team seemed to regard them as second-class citizens. Calls were always scheduled according to what was convenient for the Polish side, not considering the 3½- to 4½-hour time difference or holidays in India. Additionally, the Indians felt that the Poles were cold and unfriendly toward them, as if they were people to delegate tasks to and check up on, not colleagues worthy of getting to know. When the Indian team members tried to make a personal connection by talking about family, private life, or even food, the Polish team members would respond in a cursory, disinterested way, like the relationship didn't matter and all that was important was the work itself. Of course, the Indians also cared about their work, but they found it hard to collaborate in the absence of a human connection with these strangers. The virtual nature of their communication made interactions even more distanced, and trust much more difficult to achieve.

For Nalini, this presented a significant challenge. Although she felt that she implicitly understood the Indian perspective as someone with Indian cultural heritage herself, this insight only took her so far. She fretted that if these issues continued to fester, they would not only lead to hard feelings, but imperil the project—and with it, her own leadership prospects. And as she finally gave up her search of the refrigerator and ordered takeout for dinner, she vowed to improve the group dynamics once and for all.

Thus far, we've talked about global bonding primarily from the perspective of one-on-one relationships. But of course, people often spend their time working on global teams, too. So, how can we use the insights in this book to improve relationship building at the team level?

IDENTIFY CULTURAL BROKERS

Luckily, we have some excellent guidance from Andy's colleague Sujin Jang, a professor of organizational behavior at INSEAD in France, who has studied the conditions that lead to effective multicultural teams. One of her biggest insights is that the very best teams are those that can leverage what she calls "cultural brokers"—people on the team who can bridge cultural gaps and manage cross-cultural conflict. Interestingly, Sujin found that cultural brokers don't necessarily need to be "cultural insiders" or people from one of the key cultures on the team. They can also be "cultural outsiders"—globally savvy professionals who have deep cross-cultural experience, not necessarily with the cultures on the team. In two major studies—an archival study of over 2,000 multicultural teams and an experiment involving 83 multicultural teams with different cultural compositions—Sujin found that when a team had at least one cultural broker of either type, it became more effective at achieving its goals, which in the case of her study was to enhance creativity on a project.[1]

CREATE INITIAL CONDITIONS FOR SUCCESS

Building upon Sujin's work, we noticed in our own interviews with professionals around the world that cultural brokerage can be further described as a series of key, discrete roles that people can play on a global team to enhance the group's capacity for relationship building and trust. First, let's consider that a cultural broker has many different potential points of leverage in helping to increase trust and relationship development on a global team. And the first point of leverage happens before the group actually exists: in the planning and design of the group itself.

As it happens, Andy's mentor during his PhD program at Harvard was another leading expert on designing groups and teams.[2] Richard Hackman argued that it mostly comes down to setting the right "initial conditions" for success; just like with a rocket, you can't do much once a group has already launched to successfully impact its trajectory and outcome. In a global team setting, this would mean things like making sure that members have a shared task, that it's clear who is on the team and who is not, that the group membership is stable, and that expectations for the team are articulated. And you'd ideally have a few of Sujin's cultural brokers on board at the outset, too.

What could Nalini have done in advance about this first factor—the planning and design of the team? Of course, it would be critical for her to make sure it is clear who is on the team and who is not—but that doesn't seem to be a major problem so far. What is a problem is the lack of a shared team goal with strong buy-in from each side—something we cover next in Hackman's second condition for team success.

ARTICULATE A COMPELLING DIRECTION

The second key characteristic Hackman proposes is a compelling direction. Teams need a sense of purpose to direct their efforts and energy toward a common goal. He argues that for a purpose to be compelling, it needs to be challenging—though not so challenging that the team feels incapable of performing it successfully. The task itself also must be very clear and understood by all, or the purpose will not be convincing and motivating. Finally, the purpose needs to matter—it needs to be something meaningful to the individuals on the team.

What could Nalini do now to enhance the compelling direction of her team? Chances are that the tasks and deadlines are reasonably clear. However, she could also connect the project to the big-picture goals of the company or emphasize how this is the perfect combination of people to achieve it. And she could explain how the greater organization values collaboration across cultures and that working on this global team will strengthen each team member's own skill development and standing in the company. The point here is one of motivation. Especially when cultural differences can create potential confusion, uncertainty, and misunderstanding, it's important for a team leader to create a compelling direction that unifies the team and serves as a catalyst for extra motivation and effort.

ESTABLISH AN ENABLING TEAM STRUCTURE

Hackman's third condition is an enabling team structure, which includes the number of people on the team (specifically, that it is not too large), how it is coordinated, and the norms for behavior. People need to understand the ground rules for operating together successfully. Of course, this is true on any team, but it's especially critical on a global team, because you can't assume that what is considered professional or effective in one culture translates to another.

As we saw, Nalini's teams had clashing views about feedback, timeliness, and the directness or indirectness of communication. These styles are connected to deeply held cultural values, so they are sticky and hard to change. For example, Indians' tendency to avoid direct negative feedback with a boss is not because they don't want to do a good job. Quite the opposite: their avoidance of negative feedback and conflict is rooted in their reverence of and deference toward authority. They want to do the right thing and be appropriate—that's exactly why they avoid negative feedback.

The Polish side, too, had every reason culturally to believe that their approach was correct. To them, being on time was connected to ideas about reliability—following through on what you said that you would do. They also wanted to avoid ambiguity and maintain consistency in their processes, and forthright, transparent communication was a key way to achieve this. For them, doing the opposite felt counterproductive and unpredictable. The result was a tug of war over whose preferences would win out.

You can see why leaders of global teams need to have expertise in learning to avoid or at least mitigate conflict by explaining these differences ahead of time—and how cultural brokers would come in very handy here. Each side needs to understand not only the typical behavior from the other culture, but also the underlying logic (and of course, the fact that not every person from a given culture will exhibit the prototypical behavior or buy into the cultural logic). But beyond merely explaining these differences to both sides, leaders also may need to determine the agreed-upon protocol everyone will follow.

What could Nalini do to promote an enabling team structure? One clear improvement would be to articulate a set of norms—especially for key behaviors like giving feedback. For example, it's possible that the company itself has a strong belief that a more direct style is essential so that employees closest to the work can be empowered to quickly escalate critical issues. This would be an example of an overarching cultural norm dictated by the values and priorities of the organization. It's also important to note here that by *not* articulating the norms, you're passively making a decision that may likely result in chaos and misunderstanding.

PROMOTE A SUPPORTIVE GROUP CONTEXT

A supportive group context is Hackman's fourth key consideration for building a global team. Teams don't exist in a vacuum—they are part of an organization. As such, they depend on their leaders to navigate the larger organizational network to leverage tools, resources, information, and assets that can help improve their chances for success.

What could Nalini do to create a supportive context for her group? It's likely that she could use her own social and political capital within the organization to secure funding for cultural training and in-person meetings and events, which could serve as catalysts for building trust and familiarity across the two units outside the realm of virtual meetings and email chains.

PROVIDE COMPETENT COACHING

Finally, the last key condition in Hackman's model is competent coaching. Interestingly, Hackman and his colleague Ruth Wageman found that coaching on its own isn't enough. To benefit from even the most talented coach, a team needs to be structured well to begin with. In other words, if you take a poorly designed team without a compelling purpose and direction and without a strong, enabling structure, the coaching will likely fall flat. On the other hand, with these key structural features mostly in place, excellent coaching could make the team truly shine.

Nalini could provide coaching to help the two groups work out their differences, understand each other's relationship logic, and develop opportunities to meet and discover shared interests, all in the service of building a foundation of trust. She also could use coaching to identify and groom cultural brokers and connectors on the team to help continue the work of bringing the team together to reach its potential, even when the coach wasn't around. And lastly—it might be worthwhile for Nalini herself to receive coaching. This is her first big attempt at leading a global team, and she would likely benefit from guidance as well.

We think these insights from Sujin Jang and Richard Hackman could help Nalini navigate the forest of frustration and bewilderment that she finds herself in and promote the conditions for her Indian and Polish team members to forge effective global bonds.

Now it is your turn. The following is a recap of the key ideas we've presented, beginning with Richard Hackman's five conditions for team success, plus Sujin Jang's insight on leveraging cultural brokers, followed by a short thought exercise:

1. Create initial conditions for success.

2. Articulate a compelling direction for the team.

3. Enable the team structure.

4. Promote a supportive group context.

5. Provide competent coaching.

6. Identify potential cultural brokers—whether cultural insiders or cultural outsiders.

A THOUGHT EXERCISE

- If you have worked on a global team, consider Hackman's five conditions and try to apply them to your experience.

- Was the leader of this team (perhaps you) able to put all five into place? If so, did that lead to a successful outcome?

- If not, where was the gap in effectiveness, and how did it occur?

- Who could potentially serve as a cultural broker on your team?

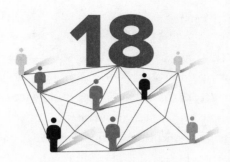

KEEPING DISAGREEMENTS FROM SPILLING INTO CONFLICTS

A s Clara walked down the hall and into the elevator at the corporate headquarters of her multinational company, she felt confident that the cross-cultural collaboration training she had prepared was going to be a major hit. As one of the most experienced HR professionals in the talent management function of the organization, Clara had run hundreds of global trainings with people from many different backgrounds. This particular one was with a group of senior managers from different functions and cultures who didn't know each other—and that, in part, was the point of the training: to break the ice, make introductions, and discuss best practices in global collabo-ration. And hopefully to generate a warm vibe and maybe even some smiles, too.

The first exercise of the day was the yarn toss—a powerful interactive activity she had done successfully countless times. The idea is that one person starts with a full ball of yarn and tosses it to someone across the circle. That person catches the ball and states their name and a fact about themselves, then holds onto the end of the yarn and throws the remaining ball to someone else, and the process repeats. The end result is a visible, vibrant tapestry of connection in the group.

Clara loved this exercise and thought the session that day went especially well. That is, until she received a knock on her door an hour later. Actually—it wasn't really a knock. It was more of a pound or a thump.

The visitor was Philippe, an older French senior manager who Clara had known to be a bit curmudgeonly—but she hadn't previously had much personal interaction with him. That clearly was going to change.

"How could you demean and humiliate me and everyone in there?" Philippe screamed.

"You made us look like children. You took advantage of your role. That was completely disrespectful of you!" Philippe contin-ued, "Your idea was ludicrous—and so typically *American*. You think everything is possible, but it's not." He was obviously furi-ous. Clara had never experienced a reaction anything close to this about an exercise she had done—yarn or otherwise.

Earlier in her career, Clara would have been completely flus-tered by Philippe's outburst. But now, she simply listened. She realized how what she thought was a fun, playful, interactive training exercise could, in fact, be experienced completely differently by someone like Philippe—an older, proud, serious French gentleman, whose greatest fear was to be publicly infantilized.

When Clara told us this story, we immediately thought it was going to be an example of a "failed" relationship. But shockingly, it was the opposite.

"No, it was fantastic. It gave him the opportunity to get all that out. It was ugly, but I just listened and reflected. And then I tried to connect it back to us—and even added a little humor. I asked him how we are now going to work together, if I'm so obnoxious and demeaning and you're such a grumpy person who should have retired years ago? We then both laughed."

Philippe and Clara never grew close, but the disagreement also didn't escalate into a major emotional, dysfunctional conflict. Essentially, they agreed to disagree. Philippe would still participate in trainings. Clara would allow him—or anyone else—to sit out sessions they didn't feel comfortable participating in. Clara occasionally caught Philippe rolling his eyes or scowling at her methods. And sometimes, Clara just rolled her eyes and smiled right back.

In any relationship—cross-cultural or not—disagreements are inevitable because each person has their own opinions, values, and perspectives. It's completely normal—and healthy— to disagree from time to time because it allows each person to express their perspectives, learn from each other, and ideally even strengthen the bond. The problem is not entering into disagreement in the first place, but whether and how you come out on the other side.

Whereas a disagreement is a difference in opinion or perspective, conflict is something else. It occurs when strong emotions and entrenched positions are added to the mix. In a conflict, you typically feel very strong negative emotions. Your pride is hurt.

You're angry. You're ashamed or deeply embarrassed. You feel disrespected. And as a result, you likely don't explore your differences in a curious, collaborative manner. Instead, you accuse; you say tactless things you know you will regret later, but that just fly out of your mouth. The relationship becomes strained and even potentially damaged. Conflicts are things you ideally want to avoid—or at least you want to create a robust basis for the relationship so that any conflict that does occur happens in the context of a solid connection that can withstand the tension.

For building bonds across cultures, then, the key question is how to handle disagreements in a way that avoids or minimizes damaging conflict and ideally preserves or strengthens an already functional relationship. To be clear, this is fundamentally different from either trying to be perfect and avoid mistakes or walking on eggshells all the time so that you don't upset anyone from another culture. In a way, it's both easier and harder than these—and it involves your mindset as well as your choices. So, now the question is: How can you do that?

The approach we recommend entails sending three different but interrelated messages to the person you're forging the bond with. These messages are important signals about you, the other person, and the relationship—which, when used together, can act as a stabilizing mechanism that keeps the teetering ship from capsizing.

MESSAGE 1
I Value You

Message 1 is that *I value you*. And this can be sent in a multitude of ways. It could be *I value your culture*—I care about where you come from; I'm curious to learn more and ask questions and really pay attention. Or it could mean *I value your perspective*. I'm inquisitive. I listen very carefully and thoughtfully, I paraphrase back your message to make sure I understand your perspective and needs, and maybe I even ask follow-up questions. The point is that I don't just lazily go through the motions on autopilot. I really value what you have to say, and I want to understand it (even if I don't necessarily agree). Another message is *I value your time*—perhaps by accommodating the approach to time that is more comfortable for you (like starting and finishing promptly or doing the opposite and letting the conversation breathe). Of course, ideally, you communicate Message 1—*I value you*—in multiple simultaneous ways well before the disagreement happens, so it's heard often and reinforced. But it's especially important when critical moments arise. That's the first leg of the three-pronged approach for strengthening a relationship and preventing disagreement from becoming conflict.

MESSAGE 2
I Value Myself

Message 2 is that *I value myself*. That might sound odd, but it's critical, because without it, you might capitulate to the needs of the other person without considering your own. This is especially important if you think that meeting the other person's expectations equates with perfect culture-crossing. But if you think about it, just capitulating isn't really what relationships are about, even in your own culture. Moreover, if you don't somehow express your own needs, you also deprive the other person of an important chance to understand you and deepen their connection with you. And so, it's important to bring this self-respect and agency to your cross-cultural relationships, too. For example, in Clara's disagreement with Philippe, she didn't abandon her yarn exercise. It was one of her favorites and (mostly) effective as well. Instead, she found a compromise that enabled people to opt into or out of the exercise of their own free will. It preserved her needs while at the same time respecting those of the other people.

MESSAGE 3
I Value the Relationship

Message 3 is that *I value the relationship*. Recall what Clara said at the end of the story: "I asked him how we are now going to work together, if I'm so obnoxious and demeaning and you're such a grumpy person who should have retired years ago?" She clearly used humor here—and chose a style that landed well in the situation, according to her retelling of the story. But more importantly to Message 3, she framed the comment as being about "us"—about the joint goal that they have of being able to work effectively together. This is the thread that weaves Message 1 and Message 2 together and ties it in a knot (or if you like, a bow). And by doing that, she implicitly communicated the value and importance she placed on the relationship itself.

In the case of Clara and Philippe, the "negotiation" was an outward, loud, even passionate verbal one. And that may be because of the French culture, which generally allows for such an assertive, direct, argumentative style of disagreement. It also could have been because the personalities of the two individuals involved were consistent with that style, too. But similar messages can be sent in other ways as well. The idea is to customize your approach and delivery in a way that makes sense for you, the other person, and the context.

We're guessing that if you work with people—like we do—you occasionally find yourself in situations where you disagree about something, and want or need to navigate that disagreement productively, so that it doesn't career off the cliffs of conflict. In Figure 18.1, we provide a chance to think through that kind of situation, using our handy diagram and thought exercise:

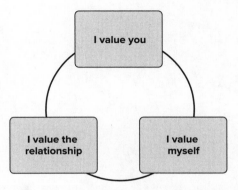

FIGURE 18.1   The three critical messages to stabilize a relationship.

A THOUGHT EXERCISE

- Consider a time when you had a disagreement with someone—anyone, really, but especially from a different culture.

- If you could go back in time, what would you say for Message 1—how you value them?

- What would you say about Message 2—how you value yourself?

- And how would you communicate that you respect and value the relationship—Message 3?

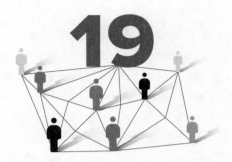

19

STEPPING INSIDE
YOUR EXPERIENCE

We begin this chapter with a quotation from Søren Kierkegaard:

Imagine a pilot and assume that he has passed every examination with distinction, but that he has not as yet been at sea. Imagine him in a storm; he knows everything he ought to do, but he has not known before how terror grips the seafarer when the stars are lost in the blackness of night; he has not known the sense of impotence that comes when the pilot sees the wheel in his hand become a plaything for the waves; he has not known how the blood rushes to the head when one tries to make calculations at such a moment; in short, he has no conception of the changes that take place in the knower when he has to apply his knowledge.[1]

As you are by now very well aware, this book is about building professional relationships across cultures. And thus far, we've focused heavily on the "building" part—that is, the things you can say or do to increase the odds of a positive connection with a colleague who comes from a different background. In this chapter we want to take a brief commercial break from these "externally focused" approaches and zoom in on what it can feel like "internally"—from an emotional perspective—to engage in all these strategies. Just like the pilot in the parable needs to steady his mind to keep the ship upright, you, too, will need to maintain a solid, even-keeled mindset to actually put into place everything we're suggesting in real life, with real people.

How, exactly, can you do that? As luck would have it, Andy has conducted academic research into how people manage the process of stepping outside their comfort zones, and he has explained what this looks like in practice as part of his earlier books, *Global Dexterity* and *Reach*. Melissa has focused her training and coaching work on this aspect of the experience as well. So, you're in good hands.

The first thing to understand is that a range of psychological challenges can sometimes shade your experience of building relationships across cultures. Although you might not feel the sheer terror of Kierkegaard's pilot in the quotation at the beginning of this chapter, you might still find yourself feeling overwhelmed, confused, or even frustrated at times—especially if you are working with a culture, personality, or context that is unfamiliar to you and the stakes are high. It is completely normal—and very human. Knowing what these psychological challenges are, and naming them, can sometimes defuse their power. Next, we explore two of the most common ones: *authenticity* and *competence*, along with emotional challenges to relationship building.

AUTHENTICITY

One of the most common psychological challenges people experience when they work across cultures is a threat to their sense of authenticity. This is because it just doesn't feel natural or comfortable to act in a way that runs against the grain of how you'd ordinarily act. And while this is true in any situation, it can be particularly problematic when it comes to forging bonds, because relationships require us to be our real selves, at least on some level.

For example, look at this quote from a Bulgarian professional in one of Andy's research studies who was trying to learn to make American-style small talk in the United States. Listen to how uncomfortable and inauthentic he recalls feeling:

> It was uncomfortable, it did not feel natural, and I was wondering if the person I was talking to saw that in me. I tried to behave like it was an ordinary behavior for me to have a cheerful small talk conversation. . . . However, I felt that I was acting throughout the entire conversation. It just did not feel natural.

A Nigerian professional in the United States faced a similar challenge to her authenticity when trying to make a positive impression during a conversation with a potential employer:

> It felt strange and uncomfortable . . . like I was disappointing my parents and my heritage by going so much against my upbringing and the accepted social and cul-

tural norms in my society. I felt like a phony, pretending to be what I was not, wearing a big plastic smile, and forcing myself to be calm when all my instincts were to flee.

You can see not only the feelings of inauthenticity here, but also the strong negative emotions weighing heavily on these two people and others like them. And while they might be able to perform out of character for the moment—for instance, in the act of applying for a job—it would be very difficult to sustain as they attempt to execute relationship-building strategies over the medium or long term.

COMPETENCE

A second challenge people often face is a threat to their sense of competence. This is the idea that people feel like they aren't "good" at the new behavior (and perhaps that their incompetence is on display to others—that it's visible, and thus embarrassing). This is particularly troubling for global professionals, because competence is one of the most valuable forms of currency in the workplace. And most people got to where they are in their careers by being competent—not the opposite—so it is often an unfamiliar and disorienting experience as well. But for our purposes, it can also stymie your relationship-building efforts if you feel like you can't do it right. Nobody wants to feel inept when it comes to their social skills!

One example comes from an American global program manager who was recently tapped to join the sales team on her organization's site visits to potential clients and business partners in the Middle East. She is personally excited by the prospect, but also unnerved. As she explains:

> Last time, one of my local contacts gave me unsolicited feedback that I need to be confident—that nobody will take me seriously as a woman unless I speak more force-fully, like a boss. This was totally out of left field because I am perfectly confident. But talking the way he sug-gested . . . in stern, authoritarian tones . . . that's another story. I am used to smiling and being relatable! It would be easier for me to adopt a new accent than to speak harshly.

Another example comes from a culture that is more trans-actional and direct, dealing with one that is relational and less direct:

> I get that some cultures need to be "nicey-nice" to main-tain harmony and build trust. But to me, forging a bond and tiptoeing around people's feelings are completely contradictory. What's more, I don't know how to do it. If I am not supposed to say what I think, and if we aren't supposed to jump headfirst into the order of business, then what exactly am I supposed to be doing here?

Of course, global professionals can also have the super-uncomfortable experience of feeling both incompetent and inau-thentic at the same time—and you might have sensed some of that overlap in the examples above.

EMOTIONAL CHALLENGES

Alongside authenticity and competence—both of which pertain to the experience of trying to do the things you need to do to build a connection—there are also potential emotional challenges related to your feelings about the relationship itself. For example, you might feel frustrated or confused about any or all of the 6 P's we covered earlier in the book. You might not understand why the relationship is taking so long to develop—or alternatively, why the other person seems so intent on fast-tracking it (pacing). You might feel confused by the signals the other person is sending—or not sending—because of their personal style (presence). You might not understand whether the person really wants to develop a personal connection in the first place, if the relationship for them is merely a means to an end, or if they are trying too hard to be your friend (purpose). Any or all of these reactions can make you doubt yourself, the other person, and the relationship itself. And this is only complicated further by the fact that for many of us, professional relationships are not ones that we get to make entirely by choice.

Now, step back for a moment and imagine that you are experiencing one or more of these emotional challenges. You can see how it would be difficult to execute the strategies that we talk about in this book under these conditions. In fact, psychological research suggests that under conditions of "psychological" and "cognitive" overload (when there is too much going on in your mind), you won't have the emotional wherewithal to persist—or at the very least, it will be really hard to.[2] In fact, your main motivation at that point might be to either avoid the situation altogether or get it over with as soon as possible to relieve yourself of this noxious state. You can see how this desire to escape interferes with achieving your relationship-building goals!

HOW TO OVERCOME PSYCHOLOGICAL CHALLENGES TO RELATIONSHIP BUILDING

The question, then, is what you can do about it. And as you might guess, there is no easy, one-size-fits-all answer (is there ever?). But we do have some recommendations.

The first is to realize that you're not the only one experiencing these feelings—everyone does to some degree. In Andy's MBA class on Global Dexterity, he splits students into groups to discuss the challenges they have faced building connections in other cultures. He then has every group list a series of challenges (for example: authenticity, competence, frustration, and so on) and chart what percentage of the people in their group have experienced that challenge. Then, each group writes their results on a large sheet of paper and shares with the class. The big "aha" for them—and hopefully for you, too—is that everyone experiences one challenge or another. The reasons are different and personal, but the result is similar and shared. And knowing that often provides some sense of comfort that your experience is not unusual or weird or an indication of something "bad." And it's certainly not a failure. It's just natural.

A second tip is to adopt a "learning" orientation toward the task of building connections across cultures. This is inspired by the psychologist Carol Dweck, who suggests that with a learning mindset, you can see mistakes, mishaps, or a lack of clarity as "data" to learn from as opposed to evidence of your underlying limitations.[3] It isn't always easy to develop a learning mindset—especially if you're more prone to what Dweck refers to as a more perfectionistic "performance" mindset. If it helps, remember that there's no reason that you would intuitively know how to interact with people who are completely different from you—and your global colleagues weren't born knowing how to interact with you, either! So cut yourself some slack, and decide up front that you'll learn from whatever mistakes you make. That's a relationship with yourself that you can work on alongside the ones you're developing with others.

A third tip is to embrace "good enough." Now, ideally, when you apply these strategies and make an effort, you'll find that everything clicks, and you are on your way to forging meaningful global bonds. But if we step back and consider relationships within our own cultures, probably none of us would expect them to always be easy, natural, or satisfying. Sometimes, we do all we can, and we just achieve functionality, not friendship bliss. And that's OK. The idea behind the advice in this book isn't that it will make all relationships smooth sailing, but that it will give you the best chance of success with that particular person at that particular time, in the particular context of the work you need to do together. *Good enough can still be pretty good!*

Finally, remember that there is no one path toward developing relationships across cultures. Over time, you will learn to cultivate your own path. Hopefully, you have seen throughout the book so far that each interaction and each relationship is different—and so are the strategies that you may decide to implement as you try to build relationships with real people. There is a great deal of optionality built into our recommendations. You have multiple ways to initiate, extend, and end a conversation, as well as a plethora of strategies for deepening a connection, finding commonalities, and building trust. Choose what works for you—and remember that, too, will likely change over time.

Now, it's your turn. The following is a thought exercise that allows you to reflect on your own internal experience of building connections across cultures.

A THOUGHT EXERCISE

- Did you ever experience feelings of inauthenticity when trying to connect with someone from another culture?

- How about incompetence? Did you ever feel like you just weren't good at engaging with someone from another culture—like you didn't know what to do?

- Was there a time when you may have felt frustrated?

- Now, let's think about what you did about this—or perhaps, what you might try to do in the future. How can you apply the advice to remember you aren't alone, adopt a learning mindset, embrace "good enough," or cultivate your own path to good cross-cultural relationships?

20

CULTIVATING CURIOSITY

M ehmet Aksoy sipped his tea and tried to mask his impatience and incredulity as he listened to the presentation. *He couldn't believe what he was hearing.* Nick Sweeney, the head of the product design department and an American like himself, was pitching a new idea to Mehmet's boss, Hiroki Suzuki—a senior vice president and key decision maker on the project.

It had been a few weeks since Mehmet had relocated from Los Angeles to Tokyo to work for this large multinational manufacturing company. Part of his job was to accompany VP Suzuki on key meetings with English-speaking members of the staff. Suzuki was very senior but spoke only intermediate English. And this is where Mehmet came in: although his Japanese language skills could charitably be described as "elementary," he could fully understand presentations in English and help his boss debrief after the fact. The role sounded straightforward enough—but as he observed the scene in the room, Mehmet realized that language would only be half the battle.

As Nick outlined what Mehmet perceived to be a half-baked idea, Suzuki kept smiling and nodding in agreement—and at the end, even showered Nick with praise. "This is *really* good! Thank you very much. You put so much time into this. I really like this. We're really going to look into this. Thank you!" Buoyed by such positive feedback, Nick thanked Mehmet's boss profusely, said his goodbyes, and confidently strutted out of the room.

"So . . . it sounds like you liked the proposal?" Mehmet inquired hesitatingly, thinking that he clearly must not have understood the context because the proposal made no sense at all to him.

"No, no," Suzuki replied decisively. "This is very bad. We are not going to do this."

"But you do understand that he thinks we *are* going to do it, right?" continued Mehmet. "Especially since you had such positive and encouraging things to say about it at the end?"

"Oh dear," Suzuki replied, furrowing his brow. "I didn't mean to give that impression. I'm very sorry. Please go tell him we're not going to do it."

This was one of Mehmet's first significant interactions with his new boss, and to this day he recalls it as a pivotal moment in his Japanese education. He could easily have been frustrated. After all, in his eyes the VP was basically passing the buck and asking Mehmet to do something that he himself could easily have done. It also felt completely unlike any of the bosses Mehmet had encountered in the United States. *Didn't a high-level leader like him have the guts to do something difficult? Was this the kind of person Mehmet really wanted to work for?*

This was Mehmet's initial reaction—but fortunately, it was only a fleeting one, because it was quickly replaced by a much stronger, enduring—and more useful—response: curiosity. *What would prompt a very senior person to praise someone publicly when it was the exact opposite of what he was truly feeling and intended? VP Suzuki was clearly a talented, experienced Japanese executive. There must be a cultural code in Japan that he was following—and perhaps wasn't accustomed to deviating from (hence, the reason he hired Mehmet?).* And it turned out that there was indeed an underlying cultural logic that likely influenced Suzuki's actions: the desire to avoid making someone lose face. Mehmet came to understand that just because Suzuki's actions didn't initially make sense to him, this didn't mean they didn't make sense at all.

Mehmet's spirit of curiosity carried him through this baffling cross-cultural moment and ultimately led him to stay with the company for the next 25 years. It helped him "tap the brakes" many times to pause and contemplate a novel situation, rather than hitting the gas and crashing through an important cross-cultural relationship. And he's not alone: nearly every person we interviewed claimed it was key to their success, too. As they explained, just like yeast is added to dough to make bread rise, curiosity is an elusive yet essential ingredient for building relationships across cultures.

There is quite a bit of psychological research on the topic, too. One of the most well-known theories is Carnegie Mellon decision scientist George Loewenstein's "information gap" theory, which suggests that curiosity emerges from uncertainty—from the experience of not knowing or understanding something and then having to figure it out.[1] It is an itch we need to scratch to relieve ourselves of that uncomfortable state of not knowing.

Mehmet had an itch—the perplexing behavior of his boss. And he felt compelled to get to the bottom of it, especially because it might happen again. But sometimes we have the opposite reaction: we are faced with something we don't understand and decide to avoid it—to flee—in other words, to do the exact opposite of displaying curiosity. Andy remembers feeling that way the first time he went abroad, to live in Spain during his third year of university. As he recalls:

> I was uncomfortable with the language, and I was intimidated in social contexts where I didn't know what was going on—so I avoided Spanish life instead of becoming curious about it. Practically speaking, I ended up hanging out with Americans at American or British pubs. *My experience in Spain wasn't very Spanish.*
>
> After college, I had a second experience living abroad—this time in Paris—and vowed to let curiosity rule the day. Instead of avoiding situations outside my comfort zone, I approached them. A memorable one occurred during my second week, when I took a trip to Normandy with a large group of French people. The experience was full of immersion activities—dinners, walks, visits to local restaurants and stores, game nights—and although I didn't understand every word, I was curious to understand and learn as much as I could.
>
> One night, for example, we had something for dinner that kind of looked like chicken, but clearly wasn't chicken. I was hesitant to eat it, but . . . *when in Rome, as they say* . . . And all I could get from my new French friends was that we were eating "*caille.*" This, by the way, was in an era before smartphones, so I couldn't just google translate it. I remember getting back to my apartment after the weekend, making a beeline for my trusty

French-English dictionary, and frantically looking up the word *caille* to discover at last what I had eaten.

I was curious this weekend—and during the rest of the year I spent in France. I constantly found myself in situations like this, where there was something I didn't expect, and I had that itch Loewenstein talks about to get to the bottom of it and learn more. (Oh—you're probably curious about what *caille* was? It turned out to be quail—the first and last time I have eaten it!)

Curiosity clearly made Andy's second international experience much more dynamic, engaging, and meaningful. The same applies to building relationships across cultures. If you have a drive to discover and learn about things you don't already know, each person you meet from a different culture presents a chance to deepen your knowledge—not just about them, but about another corner of the organization or the world at large. It will help you avoid stereotyping at the outset, because you'll remember that there is likely more than meets the eye, or that fits your preconceived assumptions. But it will also help you as you deepen your connections, because we often learn new and sometimes surprising things about people as we evolve from introducing ourselves to becoming acquaintances to even becoming close colleagues or friends. Curiosity is like oxygen or water that helps fledgling relationships grow and even flourish.

A curious mindset can also activate others' interest in you. When you appear genuinely curious about their culture, you send a very positive message: you respect them; you respect where they come from; you respect a place, a people, and a history that they identify with. You're also putting them in the role of a teacher or expert about a subject they enjoy and care about, which can be fun and rewarding. (Imagine someone asking you about a city you really know well and care about!) And while it doesn't always happen, it can trigger a positive cycle where they now feel motivated to express genuine, respectful interest in *you*, too.

So, given the benefits of curiosity, what can you do to increase the odds that your mind heads in that direction (and away from avoidance, frustration, and anger)? Following are six ways to engage your curiosity to forge positive relationships.

CREATE OPPORTUNITIES FOR SERENDIPITY AND EXPLORATION

One of Melissa's Viennese colleagues has an approach that she calls "planned spontaneity"—a phrase that sounds like an oxymoron but is apt when it comes to crossing cultures. On the one hand, you want to be open to delightful surprises and new experiences, but on the other hand, it helps to be intentional about making space for novelty to unfurl.

Melissa tried this out when she lived in Krakow. She and her husband made a point to alternate their routes whenever possible while they conducted their errands on foot. And they never knew what they might discover just around the corner! It might be a shop selling sunflower seed cookies, a castle with a dragon, or an historical marker about an event unfamiliar to them—which they could then look up and learn more about. Each meander not only helped them get better acquainted with *this particular culture*, but also trained their minds to embrace serendipity—an approach they could transfer to working with people from practically any culture.

But you don't have to live abroad to do this yourself. It's the same philosophy as going to a physical bookstore and browsing the shelves or going to a library looking for a particular book, but then becoming inspired by the other books you happen to see there. Have a wide-angle lens on the world instead of a narrow, focused lens, and you are bound to see more.

MAKE CURIOSITY A "REQUIREMENT"

When Andy goes to the grocery store with his kids, they play a game where they find one item in each aisle of the store that they've never tried before—a new fruit, a new vegetable, a new canned good, a new bakery item, and so on. Of course, they still buy the regular necessities on their list, but this game ends up exposing them to products and foods that never would have caught their eye otherwise—and that sometimes are pretty fun and delicious!

You might try the same thing in another culture. If you're at a social event, consider trying to meet one new person for every person you talk to who you already know. Or if you're at a meal in a foreign culture, try one new thing each time—perhaps a new appetizer, main dish, or dessert. Or consider the rule that each time you visit a city, you will schedule one "free" day to take a tour of the city—or even schedule a half-day tour of the region outside the city. You get the picture. You can create your own set of rules that make curiosity a "requirement." The goal is to be intentional—to make yourself do it—if it is not something that you normally prioritize.

SURROUND YOURSELF WITH CURIOUS PEOPLE

If you want to increase your curiosity, what better way than to ride the coattails of others who are curious—people we might call "curiosity enablers"? These might be people who are extra courageous in trying new things, who wonder about things, or who seem to have an almost journalistic ability to ask the right questions to get people talking about themselves. If you hang out with these people, and you feel safe and comfortable with them, you may more easily expose yourself to something new in a different culture than you would otherwise have had the courage or initiative to try. And of course, if you happen to be one of these people, you can consider it a real strength that you can now offer to those around you.

DO SOMETHING IN A NEW CULTURE YOU ALREADY LIKE

Andy remembers speaking a few years ago with a top executive at a large Japanese firm where many engineers would travel to the United States to live for several years as part of a rotation. The executive lamented that these Japanese engineers—who were not particularly adept at building relationships in the United States to begin with—really struggled to connect to the culture. They ended up spending time exclusively with other Japanese expats and, as a result, got little out of their overseas experience from a cultural perspective.

But one day, the executive had an epiphany. This happened during a conversation with one of the few engineers who successfully developed connections with American locals and who showed great curiosity about American culture. As it turned out, this person happened to love photography and had joined a photography club in his local town. Through this hobby, he was able to meet Americans and spend time with them. These photography-based interactions eventually morphed into relationships, and he was able to integrate well into the culture. Sometimes, the best way to kick-start relationships and integrate into a new culture is to find a way to connect with your preexisting interests and passions.

THINK ABOUT TIMES WHEN CURIOSITY WAS A POSITIVE IN YOUR LIFE

Chances are, there are plenty of situations in your life when it has benefited you to be curious. Think about times when curiosity was a real asset, and apply that sense of conviction to your current case. Perhaps you remember when a home appliance broke and instead of immediately calling the repair person or bemoaning the situation, you wondered *why* it might not be working. What if, instead of assuming that something was impossible at the outset, you embraced the question mark of the unknown? It's a simple but powerful twist of perspective.

Andy speaks from experience here. In his household, he is the "call the repair person" type, whereas his wife, the daughter of an electrical engineer, always wonders *why*. She has an innate sense of curiosity about why things break and how she might discover ways to fix them. And curiosity doesn't just save Andy's family money on repair bills, but it has additional benefits, too. Each time you solve a puzzle, it uses the puzzle-solving neurons in your brain, which then makes it easier for you to tackle new challenges. Next time, you may have a more advanced starting position, since you ideally retained a bit of what you learned and now aren't starting from scratch.

The same is true with culture. Maybe you remember a time when curiosity benefited you in a different way. Maybe once, instead of ordering room service at your hotel in a foreign country, you decided to walk around town and explore and ended up at a great place you wouldn't have discovered otherwise. And maybe that gave you a fun story when chatting with locals at your business meeting the next afternoon. Or maybe you were sitting next to an unfamiliar colleague at a company training, or arrived at a Zoom meeting and were stuck chatting with the host, who you didn't know that well, but you decided to be curious about them. The point is that you probably have been curious before and it probably served you well.

THINK ABOUT A TIME SOMEONE ASKED ABOUT *YOUR* CULTURE IN A CURIOUS AND GENUINE WAY

If this hasn't happened to you recently—or ever—imagine what it would be like to explain something you know well to someone who truly wants to understand it. It feels good to be in that "expert" role—especially with a polite, curious, interested "student." So, now flip the situation and think of yourself as the student. Find an aspect of the culture that you are genuinely curious about and ask questions. Maybe it's something historical. Perhaps it's the food or restaurant culture. Or maybe it's something related to sports. It's a great way to tap into your passion for discovery and exploration and an excellent way to plant the seeds of a personal connection—by communicating genuine curiosity for something another person cares about.

We think you probably get the idea: *curiosity can be a positive spark for a relationship*. You can apply this to your own life with a final thought exercise.

A THOUGHT EXERCISE

- What are you curious about, or do you wonder about, when it comes to another person's culture, background, or story?

- When was a time that you were curious and it paid off?

- Can you recall a time when someone expressed curiosity about you? What would you like to share about your own culture or perspective?

CONCLUSION

Congratulations! You have made it to the end. The topic of building successful relationships across cultures isn't necessarily a simple one—though we've tried throughout the book to propose a range of easy-to-implement frameworks and strategies to help you along the way. In case you've forgotten some of them (which is very understandable), or if you've simply skipped to the end to have a look (also understandable), we wanted to find a way to bring our strategies and frameworks back on stage for a final number before closing the curtain and saying farewell. And what better way for two American authors than an Awards Ceremony! In the United States, we have many of these—the Oscars, the Grammys, the Tonys, the People's Choice Awards, and so on. And here, today, for the very first time, we have *the Globies*!

These are coveted awards that all global relationship-building frameworks dream about. To be nominated for a *Globie*—let alone win one—is a major achievement. So, without any further ado, let's explore the categories, the nominees, and the winners.

CATEGORY #1
The Stickiest Cognitive Bias

This is a very competitive category, as so many cognitive biases can interfere with our ability to build successful relationships across cultures. Our top two nominees are . . .

NOMINEE: FIXATING ON CULTURAL DIFFERENCES AND NATIONAL CULTURE

It's compelling to categorize people into neat little cultural boxes—so much so that it's the go-to intercultural strategy for most of us. You're from Germany and are hoping to build a bond with someone from Japan. *Easy!* Step 1: Look up German and Japanese cultural differences. Step 2: Use this knowledge to avoid faux pas. *Rinse and repeat.* Of course, as we discussed earlier in the book, this has some pretty significant drawbacks. The focus on national culture is typically inaccurate and misleading, and the focus on differences blinds us to opportunities for building connections. Like flypaper, its stickiness can definitely trap us.

NOMINEE: RELYING ON STEREOTYPES INSTEAD OF PROTOTYPES

We all crave certainty when stepping outside our cultural comfort zones. Your new colleague is from India? You can bet that they are going to be self-effacing and polite when it comes to interacting with authority figures. And they will *definitely be* collaborative and group-oriented. They must be, because that's what the research says! But what if all 1.4 billion people in India don't act the same way? What if instead there is a "prototypical" style in India, representing the average, and there is a great deal of variation around that average? In this case, you would have to enter each situation with a tentative hypothesis and then wait to discover what each person is actually like. Wouldn't that be so annoying? That's why this nominee is such a great contender for the stickiest bias *Globie*.

Before announcing the winner, we feel compelled to acknowledge "Cultural Projection" as a very strong runner-up. It's such a pain to have to step outside your own perspective and consider how someone else might interpret, make sense of, and process a situation through their own cultural lens. That requires effort, and probably a bit of research . . . It's so much easier to just kick back, relax, and rely on your own assumptions.

And the Globie *goes to:* "Fixating on Cultural Differences and National Culture"—a perennial winner! Those mental shortcuts are just so sticky.

CATEGORY #2
Relationship Development Framework
That Starts with the Same Letter

You've adjusted your mindset to avoid the bad stuff. The next task is to find a way to make sense of the information you're taking in as you interact with a new person from a different culture. Lucky for you, we've got a great set of frameworks to consider.

NOMINEE: THE 6 P'S

OK—we know what you're thinking. It seems so unlikely that all elements of a framework would serendipitously start with the same letter. But miraculously, that's what happened with the 6 P's of relationship building: *power, purpose, place, privacy, pacing,* and *presence.* If you recall, the idea is that cultures and even individuals vary in terms of their expectations according to each of these dimensions. *Power* is about who you can have a relationship with. *Purpose* is about the underlying goals of the relationship and whether people are aligned or misaligned in terms of these goals. *Place* is where the real magic of global bonding is most likely to happen. *Privacy* is about how readily people share personal information. *Pacing* is about expectations regarding speed and timing. *Presence* is the vibe you give and expect from others, especially early in the process. As powerful and comprehensive a framework as this is, what's even more impressive is how *all the words start with the exact same letter.* Is there even another legitimate contender out there?

NOMINEE: THE 5 TYPES OF CONVERSATIONALISTS

The 6 P's should not get too comfortable because the plucky, upstart framework detailing 5 types of conversationalists is a fierce competitor as well. If you recall, the idea of this framework is to capture natural variation in the population and across the world in terms of conversational style. People can be *enthusiastic* conversationalists (up for anything, anytime), *selective* conversationalists (like to pick and choose), *neutral* conversationalists (will engage, but not initiate), *reluctant* conversationalists (don't love to, but willing), and *avoidant* conversationalists (would rather hide in the bathroom than make small talk). This framework has everything you want: it's intuitive, comprehensive, applicable to both individuals and cultures (though be careful applying it stereotypically to an entire culture). The only problem here—which, we suppose in the end, is a pretty glaring one— is that there isn't any alliteration at all. The terms (*enthusiastic*, *selective*, *neutral*, *reluctant*, and *avoidant*) all start with different letters. *Oh well.*

ANOTHER CONTENDER

Before announcing the winner, we must also recognize one additional very strong contender: "Three Factors to Consider When Deciding to Let Your Personality Shine Through." You might remember the idea that in the process of building relationships across cultures, you often need to pick and choose when to "be yourself" and when to fit in. Based on our research, we proposed three factors to consider: (1) the "strength of the situation" you're in (the stricter the norms, the less leeway you have), (2) your relative status in the situation (more status, more leeway), and (3) time (over time in a relationship, you can usually show more of yourself). And it's *so* close to being alliterative: *strength*, *status* . . . but then (unfortunately) *time*, which you will notice does not start with the letter *s* (sigh).

***And the* Globie *goes to* . . . "The 6 P's!" *There's always next year.*

CATEGORY #3
Most Memorable Strategy for Deepening an Initial Connection

You have the basis of a connection but are interested in deepening that relationship. We presented a variety of different strategies for doing just that in the book. But the question now is which one was most memorable. Was it . . .

NOMINEE: DAMAR JAMES EXPLORING A FOREIGN CITY INSTEAD OF WATCHING NETFLIX IN HIS ROOM

You might remember this excellent idea to actually go out and explore a foreign city when traveling for business. The key here was how your random meanderings could actually enhance relationship building. When chitchatting the next day before, after, or even during the meeting, you'll have so much to talk about or ask about from the point of view of someone who took the time to explore and who cares about the local culture. This wins a lot of points—and for that reason—plus the fact that it's kind of pathetic to just watch Netflix in your room—this nominee is a strong contender for most memorable relationship-deepening strategy.

NOMINEE: COMBINING MULTIPLE MODALITIES OF COMMUNICATION: IN PERSON, VIRTUAL, AND ASYNCHRONOUS

Earlier in the book we described how we added a photo sharing opportunity on the platform Slack to members of our international, virtual Global Dexterity Certification group. At the time, we didn't realize how powerful it could be for forging connections, but we had an incredible response, with people around the world sharing photos of their lives, which made us all feel closer. This is something any team can do—and we didn't even incorporate that next level of an in-person event yet, which we're planning to do next year.

And the Globie *goes to:* Both nominees! These are equally powerful tools. It's hard to choose just one. And if you recall, in Section 3 there were many additional ideas for deepening a connection that you might want to check out. Like a classic movie, you can return to this section again and again.

CATEGORY #4
Most Useful Tip About Building Relationships Through Small Talk

Not everyone loves to make small talk—and as we discussed in the book, the norms for how to engage in getting-to-know-you discussions differ across cultures in various ways. But using some form of conversation to discover commonalities, build a connection, and even promote a sense of trust is quite common in many global business contexts, so it's certainly worth a *Globie* nomination! With that in mind, here are the nominees for the most useful tip for building relationships through small talk:

NOMINEE: ASKING OPEN-ENDED QUESTIONS

These questions invite a longer response than simply yes or no and, as a result, have the potential of prolonging the conversation in interesting ways. For example, instead of saying "Did you like your trip to Namibia?" ask, "How was your trip to Namibia?" It's a subtle difference, but an important one. You don't want your question to be answered with a blunt yes or no, because that can kill the momentum of the conversation before it starts. As in:

"Did you like your trip to Namibia?"

"Yes."

End of conversation.

Open-ended questions increase the odds of continuing the conversation because the other person will likely provide a lengthier answer, which you can listen to, probe for additional conversational fodder, and use to continue the conversation—and perhaps deepen it as well.

NOMINEE: YOU HAVE MORE IN COMMON WITH A STRANGER THAN YOU THINK

Look around you. If you are in the same physical location, there are myriad topics you can discuss. It might be the weather, or that huge mural on the side of the building . . . or the enormous spider climbing up the wall! The point is that small talk really isn't about these things—no one really cares that much about the weather or the spider—it's that these are vehicles for having a conversation that can (a) create a common experience you've had together; (b) potentially create a positive vibe and feeling, which is a move in the right direction; and (c) potentially open up unanticipated lines of conversation that lead to a genuine interest you have in common and the potential basis of a meaningful connection. Small talk isn't the destination, but rather a bridge you construct with the other person to get there.

———

And the **Globie** *goes to:* "You Have More in Common with a Stranger Than You Think"! Small talk has somewhat of a mixed reputation—there are advocates to be sure, but lots of haters as well. What we've found is that people who think they don't like small talk are often pleasantly surprised—because they discover that they have more in common than they originally thought.

CATEGORY #5
Most Annoying Part of Making Small Talk

In spite of its demonstrated benefits, we recognize that for lots of people, small talk is a necessary evil (emphasis on the *evil*). Even in the United States, we both know people (perhaps even us) who find making small talk with strangers to be a chore we'd rather not have to deal with. With this in mind, here are the nominees for the Most Annoying Part of Making Small Talk. Because this is such a competitive category, you'll notice there are more nominees.

NOMINEE: SMALL TALK CAN FEEL WEIRD AND OVERLY PERSONAL

You're quietly standing in line at the supermarket, and someone you don't know starts to talk about the weather. And then before you know it, you've learned she had a difficult commute to work this morning and is recovering from a breakup with her boyfriend. To be honest, we're American and find conversations like these bizarre. Imagine if you come from a country where small talk isn't common, and you have to endure this social weirdness?

NOMINEE: SMALL TALK IS SUPERFICIAL

Honestly, what's really the point about talking about the weather, or your commute to work, or last night's football match? What are you going to accomplish with this type of light conversation? Some people love it—they are social, extroverted butterflies who get energy by-interacting with others. For them, these conversations are like their morning jolt of caffeine. But for the rest of us, it can just feel so irrelevant, and even draining.

NOMINEE: SMALL TALK FEELS INEFFICIENT (AND LIKE A WASTE OF TIME)

We get the purpose of small talk: to ease you into a conversation with casual, lighthearted banter. But is that really necessary? If you have something to say, how about just saying it? Small talk can be frustratingly inefficient, especially in a professional context with deadlines and constant pressure to get business done. Or like pointless filler—a big basket of bread before a meal (when you didn't even order the bread, don't like bread, and wonder why people need to randomly eat slices of bread before meals in the first place!).

Runner-up: It's really awkward to end small talk—it can feel abrupt and even rude. You don't want to hurt the other person's feelings, especially if they seem to love small talk. But you also don't want it to go on and on (. . . and on). Honestly, ending small talk for some people can be just as annoying as beginning it.

And the Globie *goes to* . . . Well—this is a tie, and it's our first four-way tie between the official nominees and the runner-up!

For people who really don't like small talk, *all* these aspects are super annoying. But at the same time, many of us who are reluctant or even avoidant small talkers understand its importance and are often willing to grit our teeth and engage. And we may not like to admit it, but sometimes these conversations aren't that bad after all.

CATEGORY #6
Best Illustration of Another Culture's Trust Language

Trust is universal, but the way to cultivate it is culturally and personally specific. We covered this earlier in the book but wanted to double-click on it here since we feel it's such a key part of building relationships, especially across cultures. The following are nominees for the most memorable example of learning another trust language.

NOMINEE: AN AMERICAN CONSULTANT IN OXFORD

Working with very posh, upper-crust, highly educated Oxford University graduates, he learned that to earn their trust—at least early on—he had to be cynical, blasé, detached, and self-deprecating. This might or might not be a stretch for the American consultant, depending on his personality—but it's a great example of a super-specific "language" of trust.

NOMINEE: AN AMERICAN EXECUTIVE IN QUEBEC CITY

The executive (who could barely skate or speak French) got up to play hockey at 7 a.m. with his work team. This bought him a decade of goodwill with his local Canadian work colleagues. *Definitely worth the broken ribs he suffered . . .*

―――

Runner-up: We found many clever examples of people adopting the local trust language. Another memorable one was a German manager learning that to win over his American employees, he had to praise them for "small wins" and minor accomplishments, even though he'd never do that in Germany—as what they did wasn't really an "accomplishment" but was simply an expected part of their jobs.

And the Globie *goes to:* "An American Executive in Quebec City"! Nice example of winning trust. And it's just such a funny image of a clumsy American businessman stumbling across a hockey rink. We admire his courage!

CATEGORY #7
Most Compelling Story About Finland

You might have noticed that Finland makes several appearances in this book, even though it only has about 5.5 million people—116th largest population in the world equal to about .07 percent of the world's population. To be honest, we don't have a great reason for why this happened. Perhaps it's because we have a brilliant colleague from Finland who did our Global Dexterity Certification and posts amazing photos of sunsets at her Finnish cottage on Slack. Neither of us has been to Finland, seen a reindeer, been in an outdoor sauna, or attended a Finnish crayfish party (yes, that's a thing). Nonetheless, we have this category with some compelling nominees.

NOMINEE: THE STORY OF STEVEN RUDDY

Do you remember that story? Steven is an American executive who had the insight to realize that the *pacing* (6P's!) part of relationship building is very different in Finland. As an "enthusiastic conversationalist," Steven learned how to handle long periods of silence during the first few days of his meetings before the floodgates opened and Steven's Finnish friends talked his ear off until the wee hours of the night. *Onnittelut*, Steven. That's congratulations in Finnish.

NOMINEE: WHERE YOU HAVE COFFEE WITH SOMEONE MATTERS

We did not expect this one at all when doing our interviews! If you recall, the particular *place* you invite someone to for coffee has a tremendous meaning in Finland. If you invite someone for a coffee inside the office—at the break room or café—it's nice, but not notable. But outside the office: now, that's a big deal. An outside-the-office invitation means you want to be that person's friend—and not a "casual" type of friend in the American sense. This is more of a lifelong commitment type of friend—something that could understandably cause the other person to pause and wonder whether they are ready for such a significant step. A great illustration of the idea of *place* (and purpose!) in the 6 P's framework—so a strong contender to be sure.

———

And the Globie *goes to:* "Where You Have Coffee with Someone Matters"! It's such a ripe situation for misunderstanding that it had to be the winner.

CATEGORY #8
Most Pointless "Either-Or" Debate in Building Relationships Across Cultures

If you don't make a living studying global work, you'd be surprised at how vehemently people argue one side or the other about building relationships across cultures. We like to call these pointless arguments because they can feel interesting intellectually, but they don't help people meaningfully engage across cultures in real life. We have hinted at several throughout the book, and here we shine the spotlight on three contenders for the most pointless of them all:

NOMINEE: CULTURAL DIFFERENCES VERSUS INDIVIDUAL DIFFERENCES

This is a big one—and probably the front-runner: whether people have been shaped by the country or culture they were raised in (and for some people, this is more than one culture), or whether individual differences matter more, like one's personality, family upbringing, life experiences, and so on. Those who argue for cultural differences like to classify people according to the country they are from, and to assign a "type" or "style" to them, much like you would a Myers-Briggs personality type. One of the most famous advocates for the cultural differences viewpoint, psychologist Geert Hofstede, believed that the effect of culture was indelibly "imprinted" on us like a "software of the mind."[1] On the other side are the advocates of globalization who argue that national culture matters little anymore, joined by those who adamantly protest that you shouldn't put people in cultural boxes. You can hopefully guess our perspective by now. We believe that individual differences and culture *both* matter. We aren't prisoners of our cultures, but we aren't free-floating cultureless individuals, either. Instead, the way we think, feel, and act is a unique alchemy of multiple influences.

NOMINEE: AUTHENTIC VERSUS APPROPRIATE

Should you "just be yourself" when building relationships across cultures? Or should you pay attention to cultural norms and expectations and adapt and adjust your behavior when necessary? A sensible person might say *both*—that you can have each of these in your arsenal and sometimes even create a blended approach that is simultaneously effective and authentic. But here, too, the pointless debate has people invested in each side. Those in the "be yourself" camp feel that you should *never* sacrifice your authenticity, even a little bit—for how can you develop a meaningful connection with someone if you're not being your fullest, truest self? Those in the "adapt and adjust" category feel that we all adapt and adjust in our daily lives anyway. (Are you the same way with your best friends at a bar or restaurant as you would be with your boss or with your grandparents? Probably not—which reflects the range we already have in our everyday lives.) As you have likely discerned by now, we are sensible, middle-range-type authors who believe a healthy, balanced dose of both ideas is often best: be authentic when you can, as much as you feel you can, but don't ignore cultural norms when they are "tight" and important to follow.

———

Runner-up: A strong contender here is "Should Relationships Be About Strategic Benefit or Personal Enjoyment?" Those on the strategic side are realists who see that getting ahead isn't necessarily based solely on what you "deserve" or the skills, intellect, and effort you bring to the table. It's often by who you know and how these connections can help advance your career. On the other side of the equation are the optimists who believe that pursuing relationships for strategic benefit is a fool's errand. You will likely not enjoy the process; these folks will likely not advocate for you because the ties will not be strong; and you will ultimately question how meaningful it is to pursue goals that provide you with little intrinsic happiness.

We hope you can predict how we see this false dichotomy. Our view is that relationships can indeed be strategic—and ignoring that is ignoring the realities of global business. But you can simultaneously be strategic and also find enjoyment and meaning in your relationships. Think of a trusted mentor you have had in your life—was that a purely strategic relationship? Was it purely about personal enjoyment and meaning? Likely it was a combination of both. That's why this pointless debate is a strong contender for the *Globie* as well.

That said, the Globie *for the most pointless "either-or" debate goes to* . . . "Cultural Differences Versus Individual Differences"! This is a book about relationships across cultures, after all, and we feel compelled to spotlight this especially pointless debate, since *both* individual differences and culture so clearly matter when building bonds with people from other cultures.

CATEGORY #9
The Best "Big Idea" in the Book

We hope that our book reads like a recipe book—something that you will not necessarily read from cover to cover, but that can become a valuable resource for you to refresh your knowledge and solve challenges you face as they arise. Maybe you'll even bookmark your favorite sections and return to them again and again! With that in mind, here are the nominees for the best "big idea" that we've (hopefully) advanced in the book.

NOMINEE: THE GOAL OF EFFECTIVE CROSS-CULTURAL COMMUNICATION ISN'T ABOUT AVOIDING MISTAKES

It's about building a sense of rapport and trust so that mistakes mean little (or at least less) and can even become valuable learning opportunities. There is a very deeply rooted, unquestioned assumption in the field of global work that the entire point of learning about cultures is to avoid mistakes and faux pas. And we get it—nobody likes to make mistakes, and sometimes these do have consequences. But we think this philosophy is unhelpful and counterproductive in many ways. It can encourage perfectionistic "performance mindsets" instead of learning mindsets. It can lead us to think that we can't be ourselves when connecting across cultures. And perhaps most important, it misses the big-picture aim of forging bonds with real-life people so that we can accomplish our goals and objectives. And this experience can be deeply inspiring and rewarding! Our goal in this book has been to provide you with a road map to make and sustain these successful connections.

NOMINEE: PREDICTING THE EFFECT OF CULTURE ON A PERSON'S BEHAVIOR IS LIKE PREDICTING THE WEATHER ON A GIVEN DAY

It's inherently unpredictable, but we have some frameworks and tools to give us insight into what we can potentially expect. Cultural tendencies are not rules, and although culture matters in general, there is not one foolproof set of rules to follow with real people. We want you to remember that personality, life experience, and a whole slew of other factors might be just as important as the country a person happens to have on their passport—or even more important. Just as you know it is with your own style. You might get exactly what you predict from another culture—but you might not!

NOMINEE: YOU ARE NOT A PASSIVE PRISONER OF YOUR CULTURE

The truth, we believe, is the opposite. Culture is a resource. It's a toolkit. It might be a toolkit you haven't fully explored or tried out. And you might over time want to add a few extra tools to enhance your abilities and effectiveness in new situations. Or viewed another way, it's a dance, with an endless array of movements that you can choose to fit the changing rhythm. Sure, some of them will feel more natural than others, but you are never completely locked in, and neither are the people you're connecting (or dancing) with. Culture is something you have agency over and can use in your own way when building global relationships.

NOMINEE: BUILDING RELATIONSHIPS ACROSS CULTURES IS ULTIMATELY ABOUT CREATING A SENSE OF "WE"

When you first meet someone from another culture—or, frankly, even someone from your own culture—there's no sense of "we." You are two distinct people with no common history, memories, experiences, trust, or positive emotional connections. The goal of everything we've discussed in this book is to increase the odds of making this connection—of creating a sense of "us" by eliminating the "weeds" or the biases and distorted ways of thinking that can interfere with building relationships and introducing opportunities to forge new bonds.

And the Globie *goes to* . . . All of them! Picking the best big idea is like picking a favorite child. We love all these lessons equally and hope that they have helped you think about building relationships across cultures in a new, different, and useful way.

We hope you have enjoyed this book. But even more, we hope that by providing a new framework for building relationships across cultures in the global workplace, we can participate in a positive paradigm shift in how we think about culture in our modern, diverse global spaces.

NOTES

Introduction

1. Extensive research has demonstrated the connection between high-quality connections and positive health outcomes. See, for example, J. Holt-Lunstad, T. B. Smith, and J. B. Layton, "Social Relationships and Mortality Risk: A Meta-Analytic Review," *PLoS Med* 7, no. 7 (2010), https://www.ncbi.nlm.nih.gov/pmc/articles/PMC2910600/; and J. Martino, J. Pegg, and E. Pegg Frates, "The Connection Prescription: Using the Power of Social Interactions and the Deep Desire for Connectedness to Empower Health and Wellness," *Am J Lifestyle Med* 11, no. 6 (Nov–Dec 2017): 466–475.
2. Many thanks to our two excellent MBA student researchers, Donika Sollova and Mildred Delgado, who contributed to this research effort.

Chapter 1

1. D. S. Holmes, "Projection as a Defense Mechanism," *Psychological Bulletin* 85, no. 4 (1978): 677–688, https://doi.org/10.1037/0033-2909.85.4.677.
2. See, for example, P. Ekman, "Darwin, Deception and Facial Expression," in *Emotions Inside Out: 130 Years After Darwin's "The Expression of the Emotions in Man and Animals,"* eds. P. Ekman, R. J. Davidson, and F. De Waals, *Annals of the New York Academy of Sciences*, vol. 1000 (New York: New York Academy of Sciences, 2003), 205–221.
3. D. Kahneman, *Thinking, Fast and Slow* (Farrar, Straus, and Giroux, 2011).

Chapter 8

1. N. Ambady and R. Rosenthal, "Thin Slices of Expressive Behavior as Predictors of Interpersonal Consequences: A Meta-Analysis," *Psychological Bulletin* 111, no. 2 (1992): 256–274, https://doi.org/10.1037/0033-2909.111.2.256.

Chapter 10

1. N. Ambady, F. J. Bernieri, and J. A. Richeson, "Toward a Histology of Social Behavior: Judgmental Accuracy from Thin Slices of the Behavioral Stream," *Advances in Experimental Social Psychology* 32 (2000): 201–271.

Chapter 13

1. D. M. Wegner et al., "Paradoxical Effects of Thought Suppression," *Journal of Personality and Social Psychology* 53, no. 1 (1987): 5–13, https://doi.org/10.1037/0022-3514 .53.1.5.
2. M. J. Gelfand et al., "Differences Between Tight and Loose Cultures: A 33-Nation Study," *Science* 332, no. 6033 (2011): 1100–1104.
3. E. P. Hollander, "Conformity, Status, and Idiosyncrasy Credit," *Psychological Review* 65, no. 2 (1958): 117–127, https://doi.org/10.1037/h0042501.

Chapter 14

1. N. Epley and J. Schroeder, "Mistakenly Seeking Solitude," *Journal of Experimental Psychology: General* 143, no. 5 (2014): 1980–1999, https://doi.org/10.1037/a0037323.

Chapter 16

1. L. A. Perlow, C. N. Hadley, and E. Eun, "Stop the Meeting Madness," *Harvard Business Review*, July–August 2017, https://hbr.org/2017/07/stop-the-meeting-madness.

Chapter 17

1. S. Jang, "Cultural Brokerage and Creative Performance in Multicultural Teams," *Organization Science* 28, no. 6 (2017).
2. See, for example, J. R. Hackman and R. Wageman, "A Theory of Team Coaching," *Academy of Management Review* 30, no. 2 (2005): 269–287, https://doi.org/10.2307/20159119; and J. R. Hackman, "What Makes for a Great Team?," *APA Science Briefs* (2004): 18.

Chapter 19

1. S. Kierkegaard, *Thoughts on Crucial Situations in Human Life*, trans. David F. Swenson and Lillian Marvin Swenson (Minneapolis: Augsburg Publishing House, 1941).
2. M. Muraven, D. M. Tice, and R. F. Baumeister, "Self-Control as Limited Resource: Regulatory Depletion Patterns," *Journal of Personality and Social Psychology* 74 (1998): 774–789.
3. Carol S. Dweck, *Mindset* (New York: Ballantine Books, 2008).

Chapter 20

1. See, for example, G. Loewenstein, "The Psychology of Curiosity: A Review and Reinterpretation," *Psychological Bulletin* 116, no. 1 (1994): 75–98, https://doi.org/10.1037/0033-2909.116.1.75.

Chapter 21

1. Geert Hofstede, *Culture's Consequences: International Differences in Work-Related Values*, Cross-Cultural Research and Methodology 5 (Beverly Hills, CA: SAGE, 1980).

INDEX

Page numbers followed by *f* indicate figures; *t* indicate tables.

ABOUT THE AUTHORS

Andy Molinsky is a Professor of International Management and Organizational Behavior at Brandeis University. He received his PhD in Organizational Behavior and MA in Psychology from Harvard University, his MA in International Affairs from Columbia University, and BA in International Affairs from Brown University.

Andy's work helps people develop the insights and courage necessary to act outside their personal and cultural comfort zones when doing important but challenging tasks in work and life. A frequent contributor to the *Harvard Business Review*, Andy is the author of two previous books, *Global Dexterity* and *Reach*.

Andy was named a Top Voice on LinkedIn for his work in education, and one of Marshall Goldsmith's Top 50 Global Coaches. Prior to entering academia, Andy studied in Spain and worked for an international marketing research firm in France.

For additional information see www.andymolinsky.com.

Melissa Hahn believes that cultural skills are for everyone, and she helps people develop their own capacities through consulting, training, coaching, and teaching. She has a BA in Russian Area Studies from St. Olaf College and MA in Intercultural Relations from the University of the Pacific. She teaches intercultural communication to graduate students at American University's School of International Service, contributes articles about crossing cultures and global work to *Harvard Business Review*, and is passionate about embracing culture in her own life. She has lived all across the United States and in Krakow, Poland, and currently lives in Los Angeles with her husband and husky.

For more information, see www.hahncultural.com.